MY ANCESTOR
WORKED IN
THE THEATRE

by Alan Ruston

SOCIETY OF GENEALOGISTS ENTERPRISES LTD

Published by
Society of Genealogists Enterprises Limited
14 Charterhouse Buildings
Goswell Road
London EC1M 7BA

First edition 2005
Reprinted 2007

© Alan Ruston 2005

ISBN 10: 1 903462 89 4
ISBN 13: 978 1 903462 89 8

British Library Cataloguing in Publication Data
A CIP Catalogue record for this book is available from the British Library

The Society of Genealogists Enterprises Limited is a wholly owned subsidiary
of the Society of Genealogists, a registered charity, no 233701

About the Author
Alan Ruston has been researching his family history in the theatre since 1967,
and has had articles published in journals devoted to theatrical history. He is
Vice-President of the Hertfordshire Family History Society, having been
formerly its chairman and editor of its quarterly journal, *Hertfordshire People*.
He is the author of a previous work in this series entitled *My Ancestors were
English Presbyterians or Unitarians* (Second Edition 2001)

Cover illustration - Nelson Lee in a pantomine parts 1830's

CONTENTS

Introduction   1

Brief History of the Theatre and Popular Entertainments   3

How to get started   8

Sources for the family historian   10
    Playbills   10
    Newspapers   13
    Biographies   15

Specialist areas   18
    The Theatres   18
    Fairs and Circuses   20
    Music hall   24
    Pantomimes   27
    Ireland   28
    Scotland   29

Societies, Institutions and Specialist Archives   31

List of repositories   37

Tracing theatrical ancestors - how it can be done   72
    Richard Nelson Lee and Harry Champion.

INTRODUCTION

Everyone has had experience of the theatre at some time, be it Shakespeare or the broadest comedy. The pantomime at Christmas has always, and still does, enthral the young and the not so young. The theatre is ever with us and can fix the attention in a way that television rarely seems able to achieve. Perhaps this is because it is presented away from the home in a large and bright public place.

Theatrical performances have taken place for thousands of years, and the associated literature is vast. However what is not vast are accounts of the theatre and its connection with family history. Virtually nothing has been published, though family historians are increasingly finding the terms actor, stage manager or even scene shifter or carpenter appearing on birth, marriage and death certificates. It was seeing in the 1960s the occupation of 'theatre manager' appearing alongside my great great grandfather's name on his son's marriage certificate that set me off on my own researches in this field.

The subject is so extensive that this book can only scratch the surface. The aim of this introductory work is to set the family historian on their way by providing a guide to the sources. Theatre researches will not provide much genealogy, like actual dates of birth, marriage and death except in obituaries that appear in theatrical newspapers and biographies. Actors, and the term applies to both sexes, are usually coy about their age and often their parentage and put smoke screens around this information. What your researches may well supply is family history - what your ancestor did, or was, where he or she appeared and when. It can be difficult to find an address where they lived, as the profession was and remains, fickle, unstable and peripatetic. The names under which they appeared can vary considerably. But it was an expanding profession from the nineteenth century onwards. An analysis of the 1851 census shows 2040 people claiming they were actors in England and Wales, rising to 18240 by 1911 (both are only a proportion of those involved in entertainment), with the numbers growing massively as the twentieth century progressed.

This guide covers those performing arts dependent on a text, either spoken or sung on stage by living persons, with the addition of the circus. It includes the theatre, music hall, pantomime, variety and vaudeville, both professional and amateur, and tangentially the opera. When the word 'theatre' is used in the text it covers each of these aspects; there are no hard and fast demarcations as theatre does not just mean drama. Sound and moving image repositories are mentioned but their holdings are beyond the scope of this work. Musical performances, dance, mime, puppetry, television and radio are not included though some of the repositories mentioned can provide leads into this large area. Nor are specialist theatre subjects covered, like the London Yiddish theatre.

Theatrical architecture, design or production are not covered as these aspects are not directly concerned with family history. It may be easy for readers to say, 'why hasn't he covered this or that?'. I must apologise to them but to attempt to be comprehensive is beyond the compass of a work in the My Ancestor series. This is a first venture into theatrical ancestry and what is here is my evaluation of what family historians entering the field may find useful. The Internet will be an essential tool as new guides and indexes, and even actual documents, appear constantly; the use of a search engine to surf the net is now essential.

There are few lists or indexes of actors - it has always been an ill-defined and vague profession, poorly paid for the majority but providing great riches for the leading players. The top figures are well documented in each epoch, some over much and inaccurately, but finding detail on a bit part occasional player in a minor provincial theatre can be almost as difficult as identifying an agricultural labourer in the eighteenth century. Those employed back or front stage in the ticket office, or in making or raising the scenery, are even more difficult to identify. A carpenter employed in a small London theatre in the nineteenth century is among the most difficult category of theatre employee to trace.

Theatrical ancestry is a challenge but one that can yield much for the family historian.

A BRIEF HISTORY OF THE ENGLISH THEATRE AND POPULAR ENTERTAINMENTS TO 1950

There are numerous histories of the theatre for every epoch and encompassing the world. Those starting out on researches should read at least one at the outset of their enquiries. They are too numerous to recommend, though those written by Bamber Gascoigne, for example *Twentieth Century Drama*, London, 1962 and subsequent editions, are considered excellent introductions. More comprehensive is the *Cambridge History of the British Theatre*, 3 volumes, Cambridge University Press, 2004, which covers theatre from Roman times to 2002.

The brief outline given here aims to give a flavour of the theatrical entertainments industry over recent centuries, an introductory guide for the family historian through the mainly London theatre until the 1950's.

For the theatre and family history it's not possible to talk of the theatre before 1576 in the time of Elizabeth I when the first purpose built playhouse was erected. There were a few professional actors although strolling players had been touring since well before the fifteenth century presenting mystery plays, moral stories based on the Bible, and crude farces. Early Elizabethan plays were performed by amateurs, but the arrival on the scene of dramatists enabled troupes of actors to develop into a profession. Blank verse in which the plays of Shakespeare and Marlow were written was not invented until the 1550s. The early professional actors were seen by society as vagabonds, much attacked by the Puritans. It was only by becoming a nobleman's servant that they could escape punishment. For instance the best known troupe who occupied the first theatre in London were known as the Earl of Leicester's Men.

From the 1570s the number of theatrical performances of various types expanded greatly, with the Curtain and the Rose Theatres being built north of the Thames and the Swan and the Globe (1599) on the south side. It's estimated that by about 1600, nearly one in eight of the London population went to the theatre each week. This period saw the advent of the leading actor within the troupe, who had a close connection with the playwrights. Thus Christopher Marlowe had Edward Alleyn and Shakespeare Richard Burbage as their continuing leading actor. Some records exist for this period but these are little more than lists of players. Women were not allowed to appear on the stage as this would have been too much for the Puritans of the time, though boy actors were allowed and were popular.

The new King, James I, came to London in 1603 and was more interested in the theatre than Queen Elizabeth, so much so that one of the London troupes was known as The

King's Men. Other dramatists appeared around this time like Ben Johnson, Thomas Kyd and Thomas Dekker. The masques which first became popular in the previous century became more elaborate. Masques were hybrid entertainments, both serious and comic with music which could involve moving stages and scenes. These were expensive to mount and designed to be performed at Court.

However by the 1640s the theatre was under attack, and in September 1642 Parliament issued an Ordnance against plays and 'interludes' and ordered that 'public stage plays shall cease to be forborne.' From 1642 to 1660 the theatre in all its forms was rigorously suppressed. Performances did take place, though subject to raids by the army.

With the restoration of the Monarchy and the advent of King Charles II in 1660, the theatre was restored. It was from this period that the modern theatre can be said to date. The King was a leading patron. The new theatres were indoors instead of being open to the weather though were smaller in size. The audience was no longer a cross section of the population but consisted chiefly of the upper and middle classes. It was about this time the earliest operas were performed. Drury Lane Theatre was opened in 1663, and actresses appeared on stage though at first they were in short supply.

The King only allowed two acting companies in London, both with Royal Patents, under Sir William Davenant and Thomas Killigrew. Another golden age of the theatre arose which inspired what is known as Restoration comedy and tragedy. The chief authors were William Wycherley, William Congreave and George Farquahar, and their works, requiring greater acting skills, are still regularly performed today.

The start of the eighteenth century saw an expansion in the number of theatres built, not only in London but across the country. Three of these still remain - at Bristol, Richmond in Yorkshire and Margate. Strolling players took plays and farces around the country, travelling on foot and wagon with their scenery and props. Again the audience was mainly from the middle classes. Later in the century important actors came to the fore like David Garrick, who revolutionised acting methods, James Quinn, Charles Macklin and John Kemble. Female leading actors included Peg Woffington and Susannah Cibber.

The government opted for regulation as ministers judged that the authorised theatre system was breaking down, and attending the theatre could be a rowdy experience. The dramatist Henry Fielding mounted two plays at an unpatented London theatre in the 1730s which scored points against politicians and in particular the Prime Minister, Sir Robert Walpole. The result was the Licensing Act of 1737 which gave the Lord Chamberlain power to issue licences only to those theatres of which he approved, and to appoint an official for the reading and licensing of plays. Formal censorship had arrived. This unpopular measure had a significant influence on the theatre (it created in effect the Theatre Royal system in each town) and determined which plays, their content and the nature of performances mounted in them.

Many 'minor' theatres were created as a result of the restrictions the Act imposed. These theatres appeared because of expanding demand for entertainment arising out of increased prosperity in England in the eighteenth century. While the government limited the performance of legitimate drama to the more expensive patents, the 'minor' theatres circumvented the law by mounting pantomimes (essentially an eighteenth century creation from the Italian commedia dell'arte), concerts, or by setting a play to music so it could be defined as a burletta.

One of the 'minors' was Sadlers Wells in London which put on entertainments well into the nineteenth century that allowed for cheap entry for a long evening starting often at 6pm, consisting, perhaps of an animal show, a play by Shakespeare, a dramatic presentation set to music, music or at certain times of the year a pantomime. The later someone entered the evening performance the cheaper was the admission. This arrangement spread over the country with similar programmes. Stage settings in the late eighteenth century particularly in the popular theatre were changing and in the nineteenth century many pantomimes were written around the increasingly complex scenery.

Theatres were increasing in audience capacity and the new Drury Lane of 1792 could hold over 3,600 people. The entertainments mounted varied greatly, for example, Astley's Amphitheatre near Westminster became famous for its circus and equestrian performances. Large theatres with few rules as to the size of the audience combined with naked flames for lighting led to frequent fires and panics. By 1800 what can be described as a general passion existed for amusements in all forms throughout English society.

The actor Edmund Keen bestrode the early nineteenth century theatre like a colossus and the boy actor Master Betty was in great demand. Pantomime with its many scenes and dramatic sections became a national art form, the superstar of which was Joseph Grimaldi. The pantomime as it is known today did not develop until after 1850. The theatre got rougher from the 1820s, which matched the nature of the changing audience. The respectable did not attend. The 'minor' theatre system was starting to break up which was a contributory reason for the Theatre Act of 1843 that abolished the patent theatre's monopoly but retained the power of the Lord Chamberlain over performances. Travelling shows covered the country at fairs at which Shakespeare's plays could be got through in fifteen minutes for a simple rural audience. The circuit system, which grouped theatres in a locality, enabled troupes of actors to gain audiences on a regular basis.

The mid nineteenth century saw the rise of the penny gaffs (theatre for a penny) and the music halls in cities, often attached to public houses. The circus came onto the scene at about the same time replacing menageries and touring fairs which had been the staple entertainment medium in smaller towns and villages. Entertainments could be creative, interactive, boisterous, crude and disruptive often at the same time to cater for a mass audience. By the 1870s the music hall in purpose-built theatres had become an established institution. This was truly 'theatre by the people for the people', and an essential part of working class life. Singers and comedians like Marie Lloyd, Dan Leno and Harry Champion became national figures.

The 'legitimate' theatres on the other hand attempted to bring in a higher class of audience. The second half of the century saw the rise of the actor-managers like Samuel Phelps and Henry Irving. Irving became the most famous theatre figure of his time and the first actor to be knighted. Improved transport not only allowed enhanced public access to central theatres but also encouraged extensive touring by individuals and troupes not only around Britain but through Europe, America and beyond. New serious drama increased the range and scope of plays available, from the pens of Ibsen, Strindberg, Chekhov and towards the end of the century George Bernard Shaw. Theatre building was not only stepped up, with stricter regulation over building construction to prevent fires, but seat arrangements in theatres was also changing. For example, the traditional cheapest seats in the pit became the most expensive stalls.

The twentieth century saw the arrival of the repertory theatre, which was pioneered in Dublin in 1908 and later spread nation-wide. A different play was performed for a week or a fortnight, perhaps longer, throughout the year and generally with the same actors. The system became the backbone of the provincial theatre, and schools for teaching acting arose; many famous names learnt their skills in the repertory system. This was the heyday of the plays of Oscar Wilde, A.W. Pinero, the ever abundant George Bernard Shaw, and later Eugene O'Neill which combined with the new presentation of traditional drama by Harley Granville-Barker, created a vibrant theatre. The actor-manager phenomenon continued until mid century with figures like John Gielgud and Donald Wolfit.

On the lighter side, variety and vaudeville, which commenced in nineteenth century America, was a cleanup of the boisterous theatre to be found in most cities. It was a mixture of singing, dancing, male impersonations, comedy and acrobatics. In Britain, after the First World War, variety replaced the music hall in popular affection and support. Key figures included Max Miller, Sid Field, and Flanagan and Allen.

During the First World War audiences wanted light entertainment to relieve the depression of the time, though in the 1920s and 1930s came a golden age of serious acting with John Gielgud, Ralph Richardson and Lawrence Olivier, made more effective by the work of new directors like Tyrone Guthrie. The impact of cinema and radio affected theatre of all types and the public demanded to see well known cinema actors on stage. The plays, revues, songs and acting of Noel Coward proved to be a magnet for new audiences in the inter-war period.

The Second World War created a boom in the arts generally, and the exciting Old Vic Theatre and Company of the 1930s was brought back to life in 1944. The censorship of the Lord Chamberlain continued (not abolished until 1968) to restrict what could be performed, though the arrival of theatre clubs meant much could be presented that was beyond the commercial theatre to mount. The rise of the musical, often from the USA, with an extensive cast like Oklahoma, Annie Get Your Gun and South Pacific, proved very popular and became increasingly so after 1950. A National Theatre had been a dream since the eighteenth century and eventually the foundation stone was laid in 1951 although building did not start until 1969 and the National Theatre opened in 1975. It is located on the south bank of the Thames, not far from the sites of The Swan and the Globe where the story had started.

HOW TO GET STARTED

The word 'actor' or 'actress', or even 'comedian' or 'acrobat', has appeared on a birth, marriage or death certificate of an ancestor, and after the first excitement you ask yourself where do you go now. This will depend on your knowledge of the history of the performing arts in Great Britain, the period you're seeking to research, and the area where the performer in question is likely to have worked. You may seek to find out specific details, but that may not be possible; the best approach is to locate any possible reference and build up a picture of your ancestor from there.

As a first step obtain at least an outline history of the British theatre from a local library, or buy one and read it carefully. These are numerous but the latest version is not essential; you're looking at the past not for details on current actors. A classic book on the nineteenth century, for example, is *Victorian Theatre* by George Rowell, Oxford, first edition 1956 but there are many more in this category. Browsing through *The Oxford Companion to the Theatre*, edited by Phyllis Hartnoll, the latest edition of which is to be found in most local libraries will give an idea of the scope and range for your research study. It is unwise to assume knowledge if your experience of the theatrical entertainments is limited to attending pantomimes or circuses in childhood. Become as knowledgeable as you can before you start out on your quest - this booklet should help you on the way.

The next question to ask is where research can be undertaken in your locality for the theatrical area you have settled on, like for example the music hall in Manchester. Those within striking distance of central London have a wide choice. Westminster Reference Library, the Guildhall Library and the British Library Newspaper Collection at Colindale are major nation-wide resources which I have used repeatedly. The list of repositories and libraries given in this book should enable you to find a research source and a theatre-based library in your locality.

At an early stage determine the places where your ancestor is likely to have performed. If you can settle on a specific theatre or hall then contact the local Record Office and Local Studies library to ascertain what they have. Few existing theatres retain historical material and will refer you elsewhere. Theatre administrators are generally, as perhaps they should be, only really interested in their latest productions. If you know the date of death examining the obituary columns in relevant theatrical newspapers (or even local newspapers) is a worthwhile project. It's not always necessary to go to Colindale; copies of these newspapers are held in different parts of the country, often on microfilm. The ever evolving indexes of various kinds located on the world wide web can help further.

The aim is to build up as complete a profile of your ancestor as possible before entering on detailed research. You may of course, as I did, find profiles of your ancestor straight away in a biographical dictionary in a local library but most family historians are unlikely to be as lucky as this. It can be a slog with many of the avenues suggested in this work seemingly leading nowhere. Unfortunately experts in the field of family history and the theatre are few. The specialist societies may help; their primary interest is the history of a particular branch of the entertainment industry and they are knowledgeable about its records. They may be able to assist when you're stuck and seemingly trying to find a needle in a haystack. However like most areas of family history there can be a sudden breakthrough when an ancestor will be mentioned on a scrappy piece of theatre ephemera, possibly wafer-thin and dirty. You won't find much genealogy but you have the possibility of locating a rich family history amongst this most unstable but exciting of professions.

SOURCES FOR THE FAMILY HISTORIAN

PLAYBILLS

One of the key sources for locating an author, player or manager in the theatre and popular entertainments is the playbill. Family historians attempting to trace the theatrical activities of nineteenth century forebears cannot avoid them. The playbill typically consists of a single sheet of paper, often very thin and sometimes nearly transparent, on which is printed in large letters an advertisement for a play or evenings' entertainment to be performed in a particular theatre or hall. It was designed for use as a poster to be stuck on a wall, or to be handed out to potential customers in the street as well as a programme for use by the audience. The playbill was the centrepiece of advertising up to the 1860s and was not designed for retention.

The first poster playbills were printed in London for the management of Drury Lane and Covent Garden Theatres to be stuck on walls; the earliest survival is from 1687. Until the mid eighteenth century little prominence was given to the names of the players, and most of the cast were not mentioned. The printing could be crude, employing large letters for the title and the information presented in a haphazard manner. Often it is maddeningly imprecise, for example 'Othello... Mr Jones'. Very often first names or initials were not included making the reference impossible to identify. In the early period playbills were usually quarto sheets for circulation in coffee houses and for placing outside theatres. The playbill developed as printing technology advanced. The first programme type playbills came in the 1850s at the Olympic Theatre in London, which were small bills folded down the middle and given to patrons of the more expensive seats without charge. This cast list type of bill/programme remains available today free at places like the National Theatre.

By the 1880s the modern programme, for which a charge is made, was becoming common and contained much more information on the actors and the production. By the mid 1880's programmes were staring to appear in colour. From the 1890s very large advertising posters for display outside the theatre appeared, and under French influence became an art form; these are of limited interest for the family historian. Following the First World War the booklet type programme that we know today became the rule. Theatre programmes are a major source for family historian from the second half of the nineteenth century, but before that playbills are the key source.

More playbills exist than other types of theatre ephemera, like proclamations, tickets, labels etc. due to their immediacy and attractiveness. More substantial theatre records

IL DIAVOLO ANTONIO

AND THE TWO YOUNG DIAVOLO'S

are engaged for a limited period, and will give, each Evening, their combined and wonderful Performances.

Public attention is directed to the alteration in the Prices of Admission to this Theatre:
BOXES 2s. Half Price 1s. PIT 1s. No Half Price. GALLERY 6d. No Half Price.

N.B. In addition to other accommodation will be found many large and convenient PRIVATE BOXES, the Prices of which are conspicuously marked on each door; the Attendants on the Public Boxes have also instructions not to demand nor receive Money from Visitors; and should any incivility be offered by them, & the charge substantiated, they will instantly be dismissed.
W. WARDELL, BOX BOOK-KEEPER.

This Evening, WEDNESDAY, December 26th, 1832, and ALL THE WEEK,
Will be presented (First Time) an entirely new ORIGINAL MELO-DRAMA, to be entitled The

Charcoal-Burner

Or, The Dropping Well of Knaresborough.

"Dark, dark is the tale   "At night, when the fire burns bright,
Our Charcoal-Burners tell,   By Knaresboro's dropping Well." Old Ballad.

Godfrey Harrington, (a Magistrate) Mr. YOUNG, Matthew Esdaile, (a Miser) Mr. RUMBALL, Edmund Esdaile, (a Captain of Dragoons) Mr. C. HILL,
Poynet Ardenne, THE RECKLESS, (known as the **Charcoal Burner** of Oakwood Priory) Mr. OSBALDISTON,
Mr. Valentine Verdict, (with the song of "**The Wonderful Well!**") Mr. VALE,
Caleb Brown, Mr. ALMAR, Abraham Cole, (Hostler & Potter's son) Mr. ROGERS, Jacob Jones, (a Constable) Mr. BANNISTER,
Edith Harrington, (the "**Fair Maid of York**" betrothed to Edmund Esdaile) Miss W. WEST,
Barbara Jones, (her Waiting Woman, with a **Comic Song**, newly invented) Miss VINCENT,
Cecilia Snark, (Bridesmaid to Barbara) Miss JORDAN, Old Mother Grumble, Mrs. EMDEN.

THE HOVEL OF THE WOOD, and FOREST, BY MOONLIGHT.
THE RUINS OF OAKWOOD PRIORY, with the CHARCOAL-BURNER'S KILN.
VIEW of the DROPPING WELL at KNARESBOROUGH.

⁎ "This Well, (of petrifying quality) is situated in Knaresborough, in the North Riding of Yorkshire. It falls in a continued shower, from the elevation of a high rock, and is perhaps one of the most picturesque objects of romantic nature in the world."
INTERIOR OF KNARESBOROUGH CHURCH—Preparations for the Bridal Ceremony, &c.

IL DIAVOLO ANTONIO
WILL GIVE HIS
UNRIVALLED EXHIBITIONS on the CORDE VOLANTE.

After which, (First Time) a New Melo-dramatic Christmas Pantomime, of peculiar construction, and embracing a concentration of varied Talent hitherto unattempted on the British Stage; founded on a celebrated Scandinavian Legend, and entitled The

VALKYRÆ:
OR,
HARLEQUIN THE PATRIOT POLE, AND THE MAID OF MUSCOVY.

☞ The VALKYRÆ of the North are supposed to be three sisters, employed to weave the web of Fate:—They are represented as being beautiful, and are to be seen, by the superstitions, on the Northern Seas, before any great storm or calamitous event.

The Overture & Music by Mr. JOLLY. The Scenery by Mr. MARSHALL.
The Pantomime produced under the direction of Mr. B. S. FAIRBROTHER.

Polosky, the **Patriot Pole**, Mr. OSBALDISTON; afterwards **Harlequin**, Mr. NELSON Jun.
Zoaliski, a Necromancer, Mr. C. HILL; afterwards **Pantaloon**, Mr. WOOD,
Peter Pop, of Wainscoperi, a **Cockney**, Mr. VALE; afterwards **Clown**, SIGNOR GRAMMANI,
Yermanoff, (a Muscovite) Mr. MAITLAND, Jurka, (the Cossack Leader) Mr. MAITLAND,
Baldiski, (a Russian Officer) Mr. BROON, Sastordaac, M. JONES, Drastiski, (a Boar) Mr. ROBINSON,
Paul Lavinsk, (a Polish Boy) Mrs. EMDEN, Jallienshoff, (a Cossack) Mr. ALMAR.
Adrisna, the **Maid of Muscovy**, Miss WILKINSON; afterwards **Columbine**, Miss FAIRBROTHER,
Selwina, (a Polish Woman) Mrs. YOUNG,
VALKYRÆ, Palmora, (First of the Valkyrae) Miss VINCENT, Vaeilli, Miss JORDAN, Genie Miss YOUNG,
Immortals, Gnomes, the Fates &c. &c. Okalda, (the Scandinavian Deity) Mr. EDWIN,
Freauldi, (Spirit of the North Pole) Mr. VOUGHN, Odin, (God of War) Mr. BANNISTER,
ODGER & IRAY, (the Fates) Messrs. ROBERTS & BRENTON, Mineral Kings, (the DEMETER & CERBERUS)
Boden Mr. NICHOLLS, Woman Mr. CHIMANI, Mercury, Mr. MAXWELL, War, Mr. HOLLAND.

MUSCOVITE HUT, and ROMANTIC VIEW AT ASTRACAN.
Approach of the Cossacks, with their Polish Prisoners, on the way to Siberia.
POLOSKY, the PATRIOT of WARSAW, saved by the MAID OF MUSCOVY!
PETER POP'S ADVENTURE. INTERIOR OF YERMANOFF'S HUT.
NECROMANTIC CAVERN IN THE SEAS OF THE NORTH POLE!
Skoliski, the Scandinavian Deity, invoking the Gnomes and Mineral Kings, &c.
ODIN, the GOD OF WAR, on his SABLE STEED! attended by THE FATES, Wodin & Thor.
APPEARANCE OF THE VALKYRÆ IN A MAGNIFICENT HALO OF ICE!
Capture of Adrisna and Polosky by the machinations of the Necromancer.
ICEBERG PALACE IN THE ARCTIC REGIONS.
☞ ...."dismal reservoirs of myriads of miles of ice, the very skirts of which, floating in enormous mountains, crowned with brilliant pinnacles of every hue, delight the eye, but appal the heart of the mariner!"
BARBERS' SHOPS ON THE GREAT NORTH ROAD HOME FOR THE POLES, (POLLS.)
The original original—according under bare Poles—Russian commodities—Dandy cloaks—pulling the Cope—Clown in the wrong box.
PLANET TAVERN, NEAR THE DEVIL'S PEAK.
full of fare—bad Cooks—meat rather too much done—high game—the Venus—out of the frying pan into the fire—Satan take the hindmost.
FARM HOUSE and GAME PRESERVES near SHOOTER'S HILL.
"No shooting allowed on these grounds! Cockneys beware!"—how to tell Gloster cheese—can't hit a haystack—quite a mistake
CHEAPSIDE, anterior to its Destruction by Fire in 1666.—CLOWN'S SONG.
A lark—meeting of the Trades—great fall in provisions.
BEEF HOUSE & SOUP ROOMS—Lock's Fields Courtship; Mary will follow Robert the Milkman,
All in a bustle—fresh importation of frogs—nothing got by stealing—"Poor fellow, he wants beef!"—"enlisting for a plaister—Magical transformation of
TOWER GUARD-ROOM, and BEEF-EATERS! I don't like your charge—taking to your heels when you least expect it—danger.
EXTERIOR OF COTTON FACTORY and PUBLIC HOUSE, (Evening.)
Don't stand upon ceremony—I'll help myself—an awkward fall—killing a landlady by mistake—novel method of restoring animation.
THE INTERIOR OF THE FACTORY is seen to be LIGHTED UP WITH GAS!
Holland's too strong—Ann Twerp reduced to ashes—the light too near—unfortunate rencontre—a blow-up—

A typical playbill from the Surrey Theatre, South London

11

contained in bound books, like cash books covering payments made to actors, are rare before the late nineteenth century (or even later as many theatre managers kept their financial records secret and as unrecorded as possible). Twentieth century theatre material has been consistently collected by theatres and repositories, but for the earlier period what has come down to us is by chance, through the devotion of avid collectors of bills relating to a particular theatre or actor, or saved as souvenirs.

Playbills are found in most record offices covering local theatres, but bills for London theatres can be found in the most unexpected places. Researchers will find that, for some years, most productions are represented by a bill while for other years there is not a single item. Except for major theatres, theatrical performances before about 1830 were generally not covered in the newspapers in detail, so the playbill is all that remains. Newspapers did not concentrate on the names and abilities of performers as later became the case, which is unfortunate for the family historian. At the bottom of the playbill in nineteenth century will be found perhaps the only references to non acting staff employed in the theatre. A typical example is the bill advertising the production at the City of London Theatre, Norton Folgate for 9 and 11 August 1856 which states - Treasurer (the person who kept the accounts, a trusted figure of the licensee or manager) Mr Austin Lee; Stage Manager Mr William Searle; Prompter Mr G. Howard; Ballet Master Mr W. Stevens; Property Master Mr Samuel Walker; Machinist Mr R. Burkett; Bill Inspector (the man who among other things checked the entry tickets) Mr Squire. Sometimes the names of the Leader of the band, the head of the Box Office, and the Mistress of the Wardrobe are included on the bill. More humble people employed in the theatre hierarchy do not get a mention, but to get a glimpse into what many of them did look at *Victorian Theatrical Trades*, edited by Michael Booth, Society for Theatre Research London, 1981.

Large repositories like the British Library and the Guildhall Library have many thousands of playbills, covering not only London but the rest of the country. London playbills can be found in places well beyond the capital. Often stored in large cardboard boxes this fragile ephemera has to be handled with care; many bills are too large to be bound in books as archive material. Few holdings have indexes though their number is growing. The playbills included in the Backstage website (see List of Repositories section) are fully indexed and every name can be located. For the reminder there is no alternative but to visit a repository and to examine each bill in detail. It's always wise to ask if any new indexes have been created, though they may not be based on the names of performers. Finding aids have often been created to meet the needs of the theatre and popular entertainment degree student, not the family historian.

THEATRICAL NEWSPAPERS

Newspapers and journals, both local and national, have been numerous and of various types over the last 250 years, serving different needs. Many have come and gone quickly, some lasting just a few issues and covering little more than the events of a year. Others did not get past the first issue. These evanescent publications can be found in repositories throughout the country, sometimes only one or two copies are known to be in existence. It's possible to be lucky and find what you're looking for in a one-issue newspaper. However the major newspapers of the performing arts are the most likely to provide essential information on an ancestor. Without precise dates, locating a reference can be a problem.

The following are the main theatrical newspapers that could be useful to the family historian, and are held at the British Library Newspaper Collection at Colindale, London, NW9 5HE. The catalogue can be viewed on www.bl.uk/catalogues/newspapers. Other locations of original copies and microfilms are given though the list is not necessarily exhaustive. It's best to confirm the years held with the repository before making a visit.

The Era (Issues.1-5268). 30 September 1838 - 21 September 1939. Runs of *The Era*, either originals or on microfilm, are at Birmingham Central Library, Westminster Reference Library (WRL), Mitchell Library Glasgow, Cambridge and Lancaster University Libraries and the Garrick Club London. The *Era Almanac and Annual* (1868-1919) can be found at the WRL, Cambridge, Glasgow and Lancaster University Libraries, Mitchell Library Glasgow, the Mander and Mitchenson Collection and the Garrick Club London.

The Entr'acte (Issues 138-1968). 24 February 1872 - 14 March 1907 (The London Entr'acte 1868-1871, and London & Provincial Entr'acte 1871-1872 were precursors). Copies at WRL and Birmingham Library.

The Stage (Issues 1-4061). 25 March 1881 - 12 February 1959 (continued after 1959 as The Stage & Television Today. The Stage Directory 1880-1881 was a precursor). Copies are to be found at WRL and the National Library of Scotland. The *Entr'acte Almanac* appeared from 1872-1885.

The Encore (Nos. 1-1972). 11 November 1892 - 9 October 1930. Copy at WRL.

The Performer (Issues. 1-2674). 29 March 1906 - 26 September 1957. There were Christmas numbers from 1907-1932, which often included the dates of death of theatrical people. Copies at WRL and National Library of Scotland.

The British Library at Colindale also holds the following journals which could be of use to the family historian; the list is not exhaustive - *Illustrated Sporting & Dramatic News, The Prompter and the Footlights, The Artist, The Music Hall, The Music Hall & Theatre, The Music Hall and Theatre Review* (1888-1912), *Music Hall and Artists Gazette, Music Hall Pictorial & Variety Stage, The Music Halls Gazette, The Theatrical Observer* (1821-1876), *The Theatrical Journal* (1837-1873), *The Players, Theatre World, Plays & Players, Theatre Record*. Runs of these journals can also be found in other repositories.

The Era is the primary source for information on the theatre and popular entertainment in Britain and Ireland. It has a unique place in the theatrical history not only in Britain but also in the British Commonwealth with some coverage of the USA. It's an essential information source for family historians researching theatrical ancestors. Reviews of current productions with cast lists are a regular feature. It is particularly strong on obituaries and includes 'engagements wanted' notices and advertisements on a national basis. It also includes reports of international tours by troupes and individual actors across North America and the British Commonwealth. Unless some dates and locations are known general searches are not only time consuming, but the chances of success are limited. There is a partial index to obituaries in *The Era* in *Stage Deaths: A Biographical Guide to International Theatrical Obituaries 1850-1900*, compiled by George B. Bryan, 2 vols., 1991, Greenwood Press, Westport Conn. and London. This provides the name, including stage name, date of birth and death (sometimes the place and also identity of spouses), and the reference in *The Era*. The *Genealogists' Magazine*, December 2000 Vol 26 No 12, contains an article by P. Newman on *the Era* newspaper as a source for entertainment history. There is a long term project under way to place over 15,000 pages of text of *The Era* (1890-99) onto CD-ROM which will allow for key word searching (Keero Micofilms 320 Tiverton Road, Selly Oak, Birmingham, B29 6BY (www.the-era.fsnet.co.uk).

One of the best guides to theatrical newspapers is C.J. Stratman, *British Theatrical Periodicals 1720-1967, a bibliography*, New York Public Library, 1972. In the introduction it's pointed out that while London was, and remains, the home of the English theatrical periodical, 439 of the 1235 journals listed in the book were published outside London. Scotland had 53 dramatic periodicals by 1850 and 45 subsequent to that date while in Ireland 20 had appeared by 1850 and 12 since.

ASTLEY'S ROYAL AMPHITHEATRE.— Lessee and Manager, MR. WILLIAM COOKE During the week, THE REVOLT IN INDIA. With SCENES in the CIRCLE. Followed by the great operatic and burlesque equestrian Pantomime, HARLEQUIN BARON MUNCHAUSEN AND HIS COMICAL CREAM COB CRUISER.

HOWES and CUSHING'S GREAT UNITED STATES' CIRCUS, Royal Alhambra Palace, Leicester Square. A Comic Pantomime, entitled THE MISER OF BAG-DAD, at each performance. Clown, Pantaloon, Harlequin, &c., by the members of the company. The celebrated horse Cruiser will be introduced in his subdued state as tamed by Mr. Rarey. Ella, the wonder of the world. "Black Eagle," the horse of beauty, and the Educated Mules "Pete and Barney" appear at each performance. Pit, 1s.; Boxes, 2s.; Reserved Seats, 3s.; Stalls 5s.; Private Boxes £2 Chil...

From the front page, Morning Star, *27 December 1858*

Many theatrical periodicals and newspapers were short lived. Of the 272 which appeared between 1800 and 1850, 63 were issued no more than four times and of these 20 appeared but once. The peak periods when new ones first appeared were 1821-1831, 1901-1907, 1922-1936, 1946-1950 and 1953-1959. The Bibliography of British Newspapers lists all local newspapers by county, showing the holdings at Colindale (www.bl/catalogues/newspapers).

Press cuttings from specialist and local newspapers can be found in nearly every theatre collection, either singly, stuck on cards or in bound books. Very often they are included under the theatre name and relate to specific productions or performances. Many are infuriatingly deficient by not including the date and source of the cutting.

BIOGRAPHIES AND HISTORIES

Biographical entries for leading figures in the theatre in the twentieth century can be found in *Who's Who in the Theatre*. The Society of Genealogists Library has a representative collection, as does the Guildhall Library and the Westminster Central Library. Individual copies will be found in most major British reference libraries.

The first edition was put together by John Parker in 1912 as a successor to his *Green Room Book* which had gone to three editions. The second edition gives information on London productions and the third edition in 1916 added in *Who's Who in Variety*. Parker was involved in producing the subsequent editions in 1922, 1925, 1930, 1933, 1936, 1939, 1947 and 1952. The 1939 edition stated that in October of that year 'all London theatres had been closed the month before the outbreak of war, the first time this had happened since the Great Plague of 1665.' Later editions appeared in 1957, 1961, 1967, 1972 and 1976; some of these volumes are over a thousand pages in length. The names which had been removed by the time 16th edition of 1976 appeared have been included in *Who Was Who in the Theatre 1912-1976*, Gale Research Company and Pitmans, 1978 in four volumes. These names are contained in an index within *Contemporary Theatre, Film and Television, A Biographical Guide*, editor T. Riggs, Thomson Gale, Detroit and London which covers the world. This massive and continuing work had reached volume 51 by 2003.

In the nineteenth century, *The Era* newspaper produced the *Era Almanac and Annual* from 1868 until 1919 which included obituaries and accounts of deceased theatrical figures. *The Stage Year Book*, whose 32nd edition appeared in 1963 (first edition about 1914) also contains information that could be of use to the family historian.

Biographical details about often obscure figures who have secured a sometimes passing reference in contemporary theatrical literature in the early period are found in *A Biographical Dictionary of Actors, Actress, Musicians, Dancers, Managers and Other Stage Personnel in London 1660-1800*, by P.H. Highfill, K.A. Burnim, E.A. Langhans, S. Illinois University Press at Carbondale, 16 volumes, 1973-1993. Obviously many of these London figures had national theatrical involvements.

While not giving biographical details, directories of the London Stage give cast lists for all productions that have been identified. *The London Stage 1660-1800* is in five parts and is made up of 11 volumes published by the South Illinois University Press between 1960-1969. J.P. Wearing has done something similar in his monumental *The London Stage 1890-1959* in ten year sections - 1890-1899 2 vols. (1976); 1900-1909 2 vols. (1989); 1910-1919 2 vols. (1962); 1920-1929 3 vols. (1984); 1930-1939 3 vols. (1990); 1940-1949 2 vols. (1991); 1950-1959 2 vols. (1993) published by the Scarecrow Press. The names of the players are not listed by theatre but by play title.

Similar listing but chiefly for authors of plays is to be found in Allardyce Nicholl, *A History of the English Drama 1660-1900*, which covers each century separately. This large publication in several volumes by the Cambridge University Press, after a description of the period, lists the authors, their plays and where they were performed. It details not only the London stage but also the rest of the country. Some periods are covered in two volumes. The volume 1800-1850 (1930, second edition 1955) lists the theatres in each place, and the circuits i.e., those theatres and halls in towns around which a company of players migrated in a pre-arranged sequence. This is followed by the play names under authors. For the period 1850-1900, one volume is taken up almost entirely by the list of plays performed. C.J. Stratman, *Dramatic Play Lists 1591-1963*,

New York, 1966 covers similar ground. Michael Booth (editor) *English Plays of the Nineteenth Century*, Oxford, 1969-1976 in five volumes puts similar material in a different presentation (Vols. 1 and 2 are dramas, Vol. 3 Comedies, Vol. 4 Farces, Vol. 5 Pantomimes, Extravaganzas and Burlesques.). Twentieth century theatre is covered exhaustively in other works.

The number of biographies and autobiographies mentioning the theatre and popular entertainments written by both the famous and the obscure is enormous. Actors and managers have been prolific over the centuries in publishing their own accounts of events, often wanting to score points over their rivals, a potentially rich source for the family historian. Biographies can be found in bibliographies of theatre publications. The core work is *English Theatrical Literature 1559-1900 A Bibliography*, James Arnott and John Robinson, which incorporates Robert Lowe's bibliography of 1888, Society for Theatre Research London, 1970. The bibliography is divided into sections. John Cavanagh, *British Theatre: A Bibliography 1901-1985*, Motley Press London, 1989 follows the same format as Arnott and Robinson but is broader in scope as it includes theses and books published outside the United Kingdom. The work describes over 9000 separately published books and pamphlets covering all aspects of the theatre. The content is usefully arranged in sections, for example works on the theatre in English and Welsh towns lists no fewer than 541 items.

American and British Theatrical Biography: A Directory, compiled by J.P. Wearing, 1979, Scarecrow Press, New Jersey and London is a valuable reference tool in locating biographical information about stage figures. Names with stage name, date (year) of birth and death, nationality, theatrical occupation and source of the reference is given. For printed biographies, *Stage Lives: A bibliography and Index to Theatrical Biographies in English*, compiled by George B. Bryan, Greenwood Press, Westport, Conn. and London, 1985, is a useful guide, and from the same publisher, *Nineteenth Century Theatre Memoirs*, compiled by C.D. and V.E. Johnson, 1982, covers similar ground.

SPECIALIST AREAS

THE THEATRES

The family historian needs to gain a knowledge of the theatres or halls with which their ancestor was associated, be it in city or town. Their number, name and sometimes location, especially if music halls are brought into the equation, is often large and seemingly ever changing. Theatre names can alter with considerable rapidity, with the title 'Royal' often being added by the proprietor to make the building sound grander and more important. There is usually no Royal family connection except for the traditional London theatres. For example, the Old Vic, in The Cut in Lambeth started in 1818 as the Royal Coburg Theatre, and by 1880 had been called successively the Royal Victoria, The Victoria, New Victoria Palace and the Royal Victoria Hall and Coffee Tavern. The London Palladium opened in 1870 as the Corinthian Bazaar, then in 1871 evolved into Hengler's Grand Circue, in 1884 to the National Skating Palace before becoming the Palladium Theatre in 1910 with its third building. Some theatres, mainly in London, have their own archives but these instances are few. Theatre records do not seem to have a long life, and what has been retained is the result of chance. The systematic keeping of theatre and related records since about the 1930s is a new phenomenon in the long history of the British theatre.

The number of London theatres, halls etc. which have existed over the last two hundred years is huge, indeed each suburb in the nineteenth century seemed to have numerous halls where performances took place. Nationally one of the best authorities is *Guide to British Theatres 1750-1950 - A Gazetteer*, edited by John Earl and Michael Sell, The Theatres Trust, 2000. This work shows how many theatres have disappeared during the twentieth century. 'It was estimated in 1982 that of all the thousand or so theatres which existed in 1914, 85 per cent had been demolished or mutilated beyond recall'. Listed here are those which have survived, and in appendices are those which have disappeared, providing the theatre name and dates of existence from the eighteenth century onwards. The main Gazetteer lists the theatres by town, giving the names used, audience capacity and the architect. The concentration is on architectural features of the buildings. See also John Earl, *British Theatres and Music Halls*, Shire Publications, 2005.

For London, there are numerous lists. Diana Howard, *London Theatres and Music Halls 1850-1950*, London Library Association, 1970 is a comprehensive location list which besides architectural history provides the name and dates of the theatre/music hall licensees. This work gives exact references to the Licensing records held by local authorities and has an excellent bibliography. The chiefly central London theatres that have disappeared are superbly covered in Raymond Mander and Joe Mitchenson, *The*

Lost Theatres of London, London, first published 1961 with subsequent editions and now being revised. These two authors wrote extensively, mainly on the London theatre in its many aspects, and their works are of a high standard. Mander and Mitchenson also describe the modern theatres, though with descriptions of previous theatres on the sites, in *The Theatres of London*, New English Library London, Second Edition 1963 and reprints, now being revised. There are several other descriptions, among the best being Ronald Bergan, *The Great Theatres of London*, Admiral Books London, 1987. Books on the earlier period include Erroll Sherson, *London's Lost Theatres of the 19th century*, London, first published 1925, and Michael Williams, *Some London Theatres Past and Present*, London, 1883. For new and restored theatres from an architectural standpoint see Frederick Bentham, *New Theatres in Britain*, London, 1970. The venues of today throughout the country are described in the latest edition of the *British Performing Arts Year Book* (Rhinegold Publishing Ltd.).

Theatres with a long existence sometimes have their own published history, with descriptions of the major figures associated with their productions. Family historians with forebears known to have a connection with a particular theatre should consult its published history. Their ancestor may not be mentioned but the names of others who

The Royal Coberg, circa 1920's, now the Old Vic

appeared at the same time may give clues that could lead to further research. Histories of the leading theatres abound, and the following are a few examples - David Arundell, *The Story of Sadler's Wells*, London, 1965; Brian Dobbs, *Drury Lane*, London, 1972; Anthony Dale, *The Theatre Royal Brighton*, London, 1980; Grace W. Goldie, *The Liverpool Repertory Theatre 1911-1934*, Liverpool, 1935; and A.G. Benjemann, *The Grand Theatre Lancaster, Two Centuries of Entertainment*, Lancaster, 1982.

Regional histories of the theatres are also useful. There are numerous examples, and the following is a small selection - A.E. Wilson, *East End Entertainment, London*, 1954; G. Rowell and A. Jackson, *The Repertory Movement: the History of the Regional Theatre in Britain*, Cambridge, 1984; H. Crane, *Playbill, a history of the theatre in the West Country*, Plymouth, 1980; T. Burley, *Playhouses and Players of East Anglia*, Norwich 1928.

Town and city directories can be valuable in locating where theatres and halls were situated at a particular time, as well as the name under which it went when an ancestor may have performed there. Local authority licensing records can be found in county record offices for theatres in the nineteenth and twentieth centuries. These will provide exact information on location etc. but could require considerable research to find a specific reference. Diana Howard's book, already mentioned, provides much of this information for London theatres and music halls.

FAIRS AND CIRCUSES

It is often difficult, particularly in the nineteenth century, to differentiate between fairs, manageries, show grounds, waxworks, freak shows, fairgrounds and the circus. All were run by 'showmen'. The history of the English travelling fair goes back some centuries and provided often rowdy entertainment for the populace. Some towns had a statute fair held once or twice a year. By the late eighteenth century these could consist of numerous booths, which might present a Shakespeare play in about thirty minutes, but in other booths freaks, animals, acrobats, trick riding, clowns, jesters and anything that was exotic were on show to catch the interest of the paying public.

The most famous fair was Bartholomew Fair in London, a regular and rowdy event. By 1822 it had no less than 22 different establishments run by separate showman; by 1833 the number had risen to 33. Probably the most famous travelling showman was John Richardson who took his famous 'Show' around the fairs from 1796 until the 1830's. He put on dramatic presentations and charged more than a few pence for entry. Many famous actors made their first appearance in 'Richardson's Show', including Edmund Keen.

By the 1850s the fairs had given way to menageries out of which evolved the modern circus. The demand for mass entertainment in the early nineteenth century, combined with an increased interest in equestrian and animal performances created the circus industry. The heyday of the fair was the late eighteenth and early nineteenth century, a well documented field although not necessarily to meet the needs of the family historian.

The circus, an international activity, can be defined as an entertainment or spectacle of trained animals and exhibitions of human skill and daring. It is essentially a creation of the nineteenth century, centred on animals, chiefly horses but also more exotic creatures from foreign lands, and performers of every kind. Entertainers, like acrobats, clowns, tumblers and contortionists have for centuries been part of the British entertainment scene.

The circus industry heyday was the Victorian era when impresarios like William Cooke, Robert Fossett, Frederick Hengler and George and John Sanger, had large circus arenas. For the Henglers, see J. Turner, Circus Henglers - a family on the move, *Genealogists' Magazine*, Dec 2000 Vol 26 No 12. They also took their troupes of animals and performers from all over the world, around the country to great acclaim and made their fortune (but often as quickly lost it as well). There were also manageries, popular in mid century, run by showmen like Wombwell, Bostock and Hilton. In the 1920s the circus industry went into decline until Bertram Mills brought in an international circus at Olympia in London, which in 1929 became a large travelling tented circus. Interest in animals and human feats of skill and daring in modern times is centred now mainly outside the circus ring.

Modern British circus (in a circle or amphitheatre) is considered to date from 1768 when Philip Astley built a covered-in amphitheatre in South London for horse riding and other entertainments. The Royal Circus was opened nearby in 1782 when the term was first used. These arenas were designed to be used as a theatre and both Astley's and The Royal Circus could and did change easily into theatres. There were few hard and fast distinctions.

The circus appealed to a wide cross section of the public, from the agricultural labourer to the Royal family, centred on the exotic when animals and people were brought mainly from the Empire to astound and amuse. Circus connections were and remain world wide; at present the circus appears of more interest in places like Russia and Denmark than in Britain where its continuance relies on travelling tents. For the family historian attempting to trace an ancestor there are specific difficulties. Some performers did not use their own name when they performed, but aliases (nom de cirque). Many performers were not of British nationality and went easily back and forth over national borders. However circus posters, bills and related material can be found in many repositories.

The number of people involved in the industry is significant. John M. Turner, in his seminal book, *The Victorian Arena, A Dictionary of British Circus Biography*, Vol.1, Lingdales Press, 1995 (Vol. 2, 2000) estimates that in the order of 10,000 performers appeared in the circus in Britain over the period. Dr Turner has covered a later period in *Twentieth Century Circus People 1901-1950*, Langdales Press, Formby, 2003. The well known may be well documented but most performers left little information behind them. Circus performers often married within the profession, so everyone seems to be connected to everyone else, at least by marriage. For example the Cooke family left Britain in the early nineteenth century for New York where they married into the Coles and Orton families who were significant in the American circus. Sometimes a continuing and inherited professional circus name is the link which can also go across national borders. Circus proprietors and showmen, big and small, are usually better recorded; they started as performers and often returned to being so if success eluded them. John Turner has written on family history and the circus in the *Family Tree Magazine*, May 1988 ('Circus Family Histories'), June 1997 ('Circus and Fairground Ancestry') and *Family History News & Digest*, April 2004 ('Circuses, Circus Families and the Circus Showmen').

In the 1850s the travelling fairs were fast disappearing and managers and performers went from one activity to another. For example Richard Nelson Lee (see last section in the book) started in the touring fairs as a very young man in the 1820s as a juggler, went into the main theatre as a successful harlequin, and followed this by owning Richardson's Show which he took round the fairs with a company until 1850. He became well known from the 1830s to the 1860s for writing pantomimes for the big London theatres and elsewhere, and in 1863 wrote 'Bold Robin Hood' an equestrian pantomime for Hengler's circus in Glasgow. Lee was less successful in writing melodramas. His death certificate states his occupation as 'Gentleman' but he was really one of the more successful 'showmen' of the period, of which there were many who went from fair to the circus and to the theatre with ease. His brother James was a show proprietor in 1850 owning Hilton's menagerie. There are no hard and fast demarcations amongst the popular entertainments. This is illustrated by M. Willson Disher, a mid twentieth century writer on the subject in Britain, who called his excellent short guide to the subject, *Fairs, Circuses and Music Halls* (London, 1942), arguing that each entertainment flowed into and enhanced the other.

Family historians should consult John Turner's books which are mines of information. Volume 1 includes an A-Z marriage register section which it must be hoped he will extend - a typical entry is 'Cuthbert Edith mar. Fred Karno' which sometimes includes the artistes other names. George Speaight, *A History of the Circus*, Tantivy Press, 1980 is considered by many the most complete history of the circus available in English. The numerous books on the circus are listed in R.Toole- Stott, *A Bibliography of Books on the Circus 1773-1964*, Derby (first published 1964 but with subsequent reprints). On a wider front the same author has published his monumental *Circus and Allied Arts, A World Bibliography 1500-1982*, 5 vols. (1958-1982), Derby and the Circus Friends Association, which is comprehensive.

For the flavour of the past, consult Thomas Frost, *Circus Life and Circus Celebrities*, London, 1874, and *The Old Showmen and the Old London Fairs*, London, 1883, works to be found in major libraries which provide the names and activities of both proprietors and performers. 'Lord' George Sanger, *Seventy Years a Showman*, London, 1908 and several subsequent editions, gives a similar picture for the late nineteenth century. Circus proprietors often gave themselves a title, presumably for performing before royalty; Queen Victoria much enjoyed the circus which at its height was patronised by all classes.

The weekly newspaper for the fairground and circus industry is *The World's Fair*, which contains considerable biographical information (www.worldsfair.co.uk). It was founded in 1904 by Francis Mellor, and is still owned by his direct descendants. It's the trade journal with a global readership and has included material on music hall and magic. *The Era* for much of its run included circus related items, with obituaries of leading figures. Besides the Newspaper Library at Colindale, a set of *The World's Fair* is held by the publishers at their offices at Albert Street, Oldham and at the National Fairground Archives at the University of Sheffield. The editor is not aware of the existence of finding aids to this publication.

The National Fairground Archive (Main Library, University of Sheffield, Western Bank, Sheffield, S10 2TN, appointment to visit to be made in advance) is an extensive collection of material covering all aspects of the fair and circus, including photographs and published material. The collection has a large amount of ephemera like bills, proclamations and advertising. Its website (fairground@shef.ac.uk) is comprehensive and gives a good introduction to the holdings. Those with a specific interest in the circus may need to contact the Circus Friends Association whose details can be obtained through the NFA; their quarterly journal is called *King Pole* (formerly Sawdust Ring from 1935). The Fenwick Collection at the Tyne & Wear Archive Service, Newcastle - upon-Tyne (www.newcastle.gov.uk/localstudies) has original circus and fairground material.

MUSIC HALL

Under the Theatres Act of 1843 drinking and smoking were not allowed in theatres, but it was permitted in entertainment halls. This change did not bring music hall immediately into being, but enabled some tavern saloons to develop into minor theatres though not if they served alcohol to the audience. However in due course public house owners annexed premises alongside their taverns or beer houses as music halls. Music hall is considered to originate with Charles Morton who built his Canterbury Hall in London in 1852 (on the site of the Canterbury Arms), though the origins of this popular entertainment stretches back much longer. The history of this early period can be found in H. Scott, *The Early Doors, Origins of the Music Hall*, London, 1946.

The connection with public houses was strong, some even allowing the cost of entry to include 'free' drink; sales of alcohol allowed for profit despite the costs of providing the entertainment. Music hall evenings consisted of a range of entertainers which could include comedians, jugglers, acrobats, mime artistes, magic, dance, singers, recitations and even one act plays. While some well-known theatrical figures appeared at music hall venues, generally the appeal was made through entertainers addressing a growing working class audience who wanted chiefly low or sentimental comedy with singing. Events in the everyday life of the audience were caricatured, like weddings, funerals, holidays, food, work and wash day. Thus the singer Marie Lloyd sang about getting on the wrong train with 'Oh! Mr Porter', Harry Champion about food with 'Boiled Beef and Carrots' and 'I love pickled onions' and E.W. Rogers on family relationships in 'Following in Fathers' Footsteps.' Many of the song titles have become everyday catch phrases, like 'Get Your Hair Cut' and 'A Little of what you fancy.' Much of the material had an East End of London or cockney flavour which was the early cultural powerhouse of the music hall.

The hey-day of the music hall was in the late nineteenth century before the arrival in the twentieth century of the large variety theatres (the Hippodromes and Empires - see J. Read, *Empires, Hippodromes and Palaces*, London, 1985) which used music hall acts, and the advent of the cinema. After the First World War music hall disappeared in its original form becoming part of variety, and the American equivalent of music hall - vaudeville.

The sources for the family historian are essentially the same as for the theatre - local repositories of ephemera, specialist newspapers, books, biographies and reference sources. Music halls had their bills and advertising in the same way as did the theatres. Books which will be of value to the family historian are R. Busby, *British Music Hall, Who's Who from 1850*, London, 1976; G. Bullar, *The Performers Who's Who in Variety*, London, 1950 which includes an index of dates of death of performers since the 1880s;

A signed photograph from a giant of nineteenth century popular enterainment. Source: Roy Stockdill

and K. Ganzl, *The British Musical Theatre*, London, 1986 which includes cast lists. More general on the history are R. Mander and J. Mitchenson, *British Music hall - the Story in Pictures*, London, 1965; M.W. Disher, *Winkles and Champagne, Comedies and Tragedies of the Music Hall*, London, 1938; and E. Short, *Fifty Years of Vaudeville*, London, 1946.

The British Music Hall Society (www.music-hall-society.com) has its own archivist/ historian (maxt@hist.freeserve.co.uk) and may be able to assist with enquiries. In Scotland, Glasgow was the centre of a lively music hall culture which varied from that which came out of London. See, P. Maloney, *Scotland and the Music Hall, 1850-1914*, British Columbia, 2003. Researchers into the Scottish dimension should contact the Scottish Music Hall and Variety Theatre Society through its website www.freewebs.com/scottishmusichallsociety. Its quarterly publication is 'Stagedoor'. This Society grew out of the Sir Harry Lauder Society, devoted to perhaps the most famous of all the music hall artistes. The secretary can be contacted at bob.bain@ntlworld.com.

PANTOMIME

While music hall in its earlier years was performed in its own premises, the same is not true of the pantomime (panto), that peculiarly British institution which continues to retain its attraction. Arising out of the Italian *commedia dell'arte*, 'panto' made its debut in the 1730s, the playbills for Covent Garden and Drury Lane in 1737 being the earliest for a pantomime in existence. The tradition is that the panto commences on the eve of Christmas, and is loosely based on a nursery rhyme with fixed elements contained within it, chiefly for the delight of children. It has become a form of variety entertainment with well known names from television playing the main parts. However the modern panto is a creation of the late nineteenth century.

Prior to that the panto consisted of a story, first created by John Rich out of folklore, based on various scenes and transformations, with the chief characters being the Harlequin, the lover, Columbine whom he pursues (after being sent forth by the Good Fairy) through a series of comic adventures, and Pantaloon her guardian and dupe who has many jokes played against him. Then there was the Clown or Pierrot who was up to all forms of mischief. There were chases, practical jokes, slapstick with dances and songs and other interludes. In the early nineteenth century the most famous clown was Joseph Grimaldi who played the role with satire on current events. By the 1830s with the centrality of the clown in decline, the emphasis switched to spectacular scenic effects and harlequin and his fellows were superimposed on the main action. Thus pantos had complex titles which seemed to get longer and longer, a typical example being 'Conrad and Medora, or, Harlequin Corsair and the Little Fairy at the Bottom of the Sea'.

By the 1850s the harlequinade as it is termed was in decline, and the principal boy had arrived. By the 1880s leading theatres were starting to drop the harlequinade completely and the modern panto, that annual financial necessity for most British theatres, started to develop. Researchers into the panto need to be aware of its early format when examining playbills before the 1870s. The number of people involved in the panto was large and the main players were well known public figures. Sometimes three or four authors were involved in assembling the pantos at major theatres. The play bills are often a mass of names that should delight the family historian seeking theatrical forebears.

The panto has been extensively written about and books will be found in nearly all theatre collections. D. Pickering, *Encyclopaedia of Pantomime*, Andover, 1993 has a good bibliography, with a description of the panto today by John Morley, and a chronology. There is also input from Roy Hudd, the doyen of modern panto writers and commentators whose own works are significant on the subject. A.E. Wilson wrote several works on the panto including *Christmas Pantomime*, London, 1934; *King Panto*, London and New York, 1935; *Pantomime Pageant*, London, 1946; *The Story of Pantomime*, London, 1949. A widely available work is Gerald Frow, *"Oh, Yes It Is" A History of Pantomime*, BBC London, 1985. In any theatre research it is impossible to avoid the panto which was a large nineteenth century industry.

IRELAND

The Irish theatre has had a long and distinguished history, especially in the twentieth century. The theatre which opened in 1662 in Smock Alley Dublin is considered the third key theatre of Great Britain after Drury Lane and Covent Garden. Other theatres operated in Ireland in the eighteenth century and nineteenth century with Dublin at its centre, though derivative of the London stage.

It was from 1899 that the Irish theatre came into its own and its subsequent eminence stands along side the achievements in Irish literature, of Oscar Wilde, George Bernard Shaw, J.M.Synge and others. The Abbey Theatre, Dublin was founded in 1904 for the performance of classics, becoming the national theatre in 1924. Later the Gate Theatre for Irish and international plays, and the Peacock for experimental theatre, led the way from Dublin. However other cities like Cork, Galway, Waterford and Belfast in Northern Ireland also have a significant theatrical history. There is a long tradition of touring theatre companies, performing in small towns throughout Ireland. The Ulster Group Theatre was an allied movement in the north of the country in the twentieth century.

There are numerous works describing the Irish theatrical tradition, amongst these being P. Kavanagh, *The Irish Theatre from earliest times to the present*, Tralee, 1946;

C. Fitz-Simon, *The Irish Theatre*, Thames and & Hudson, 1963, and in paperback; M. O'hAodha, *Theatre in Ireland*, Oxford, 1974; C. Morash, *A History of the Irish Theatre 1601-2000*, Cambridge, 2004. For a specific Northern Ireland dimension see S.H. Bill, *The Theatre in Ulster*, Gill and MacMillan Dublin, 1972. The Linen Hall Library in Belfast has local theatre material.

Family historians will find bills, programmes etc. covering Ireland in the Trinity College Dublin Library, the largest research library in Eire, the National Library of Ireland in Kildare Street, Dublin and in the Gilbert Library of the Dublin City Public Library in Pearce Street, Dublin. Material on theatres in Irish towns and cities is to be found in the locality; the website Irish Theatre Research Resource (www.amharclann.ie) gives addresses and some information on holdings. This site is geared to the needs of the family historian in general and does not directly address theatre ancestry. There is also Irish theatre material in the Public Record Office for Northern Ireland (www.proni.gov.uk), and in The National Archives. *The Directory of Irish Archives*, edited by S. Helferty and R. Refausse, Irish Academic Press, Second Edition 1993; *Directory of Libraries and Information Services in Ireland*, editor Angela Cotter, Library Association of Ireland, 1996; and the latest annual edition of *Libraries in the UK and the Republic of Ireland*, Library Association, can be useful guides although there are few specific references to theatre holdings.

SCOTLAND

The Scottish theatre in the eighteenth century had a hard time to establish itself with the first regular theatre opening in Edinburgh in 1736. However, few of these early theatres lasted, for by the 1750s big disputes arose between theatre supporters and religiously motivated opponents. One theatre in Glasgow in 1764 was even destroyed in a religious riot, but a theatre culture did become established. By 1800 there were nine permanent playhouses in Scotland and by the end of the nineteenth century there were hundreds of theatres and halls operating in Scotland. The big expansion came in the period 1850 to 1914. Scotland at the same time created it own very popular brand of music hall centred on Glasgow. In 1900 there were 32 theatres in Scotland which by 1910 had risen to 53. However between 1919 and 1939 over 30 of these had closed.

Books on the Scottish theatre are few but D. Hutchison, *The Modern Scottish Theatre*, Glasgow, 1977; and Bill Findlay (editor), *A History of the Scottish Theatre*, Edinburgh, 1998 are sound surveys. Periodicals and magazines covering Scottish entertainment in the past include *The Glasgow Harlequin*, *The Northern Review*, *The Scots Magazine*, *Scots Theatre*, *Scottish Stage*, *Scottish Theatre* and *SMT magazine*. The major Scottish newspapers *The Glasgow Herald* and *The Scotsman* and the evening papers gave extensive coverage to the theatre including amateur drama. See List of Repositories for holdings of Scottish material. The Mitchell Library, North Street, Glasgow G3 7DN has part of a website (www.glasgow,gov.uk/html/council/cindex.htm) on family history and the theatre (Best Sources for Ancestor Research, Document 11) on a UK wide basis, which lists in particular the location of holdings of theatrical periodicals.

SOCIETIES, INSTITUTIONS AND SPECIALIST ARCHIVES

First contact with the societies and institutions on this list could best be made through the world wide web.

British Theatre Museum, London

The Museum and Library, situated in London's theatreland, houses a very large collection of material on the British stage. Besides a permanent display of all types of stage material, the study room at 1E Tavistock Street, London, WC2E 7PA (www.theatremuseum.vam.ac.uk) enables students of the theatre to access its collection. The main collections are the Gabrielle Enthoven and Harry R. Beard collections of playbills, programmes and ephemera, and the British Theatre Museum Collection on the London theatre.

However the Theatre Museum should not be the first port of call for the family historian as access can be difficult and visits have to be booked well in advance. The arrangement of the collection is not designed to meet the specific needs of the family historian and rather more to the general performing arts researcher. The Museum has indexes to material on specific items and main theatre figures but lacks a comprehensive catalogue or comprehensive indexes to individual performers.

Society for Theatre Research

This is the main Society which fosters research into the history of the British theatre in all its forms. The STR is contacted through the British Theatre Museum and does not maintain archives on the stage. It regularly publishes important publications of a high standard on the theatre which can be purchased through the Society. Since 1945 it has published *Theatre Notebook*, three times a year in October, February and June which covers most aspects of the theatre and entertainment.

Theatre Notebook contains extensive references to stage figures, and family historians will find the detailed indexes of particular value published in two books. *Theatre Notebook 1945-1971, An Index to Volumes 1-25*, Compiled by Olive Youngs, STR, 1977, and *Theatre Notebook 1972-1986, An Index to Volumes 26-40*, Compiled by Olive Youngs, 1990. Since 1986 a list of the articles which appeared is on their website (www.str.org.uk), but no index to their contents has been published. These index volumes are valuable tools and I have used both to respond to family history theatrical queries.

Theatre Collections in the USA

There are extensive holdings of original British theatre and performance arts material in major libraries in the USA. The Harvard Theater Collection, Houghton Library, Cambridge, Massachusetts, 02138 (www.hcl.harvard.edu/libraries/houghton/collections) houses one of the world's oldest and largest collections. The Huntington Library, 1151 Oxford Road, San Marino, California (www.huntington.org) has one of the largest collections in America. The Folger Shakespeare Library, 201 East, Capitol Street, Washington DC 20003 (www.folger.edu) houses a collection of about 250,000 playbills, programmes, scrapbooks and ephemera items from the eighteenth to the early twentieth century. The New York Public Library (Hiram Stead collection) 5th Avenue, New York, 10016 (www.nypl.org) contains similar material as at Folger covering the period 1673 to 1932.

These are the major institutions but material is to be found in other American locations and indeed in other parts of the world. The SIBMAS website described in the section on repositories will provide a guide into worldwide holdings. The Centre for Research Libraries in North America (www.crl/edu/topics) may also help provide a way into some American resources. There are several American theatrical journals which cover the history of the British theatre, for example *Nineteenth Century Theatre Research*.

Mander and Mitchenson Theatre Collection

This large collection of theatre material that was built up from 1939 by Raymond Mander and Joe Mitchenson is now located at the Jerwood Library of the Performing Arts, Trinity College of Music, King Charles Court, Old Royal Naval College, Greenwich, London, SE10 9JF (020 8305 4426, www.mander-and-mitchenson.co.uk). The Collection covers all aspects of the entertainment industry in Britain. It's particularly strong on photographs and material relating to late nineteenth century theatre. The Collection is not publicly funded but has been called the actor's own archive and they provide a good proportion of the funding. There is no charge for researching in the archive but donations towards its upkeep are always welcome. Dame Sybil Thorndike called it 'the profession's passport to posterity.' While the provincial theatre is included, the London theatre is covered more comprehensively.

The Collection has 1500 archive boxes of playbills, posters and other ephemera, and files on individual actors, together with about 8000 books. It has good runs of *The Era* (1850-1919 with gaps) and the *Era Almanac*. There are no indexes but a project is underway to extract detail from 6000 pre-1890 bills and programmes which will eventually be included in the Backstage project (see introduction to List of Repositories) and available on its website.

The Collection has very limited staffing or space for researchers, and initial contact by phone, letter or e-mail is essential. The family historian needs to find out in the first instance if the Collection has material that might justify a visit. Donations towards its work are welcome.

Royal Theatrical Fund and other benevolent funds

This Fund was founded in 1839 as the General Theatrical Fund Association to meet the needs of the growing number of actors in the profession. It was later incorporated by Royal Charter as a pension fund open to all members of the acting profession and its first chairman was Charles Dickens. It was reconstituted in 1974 so that the Fund can make grants to whoever requires support. This means that in the last thirty years, the Fund's scope of beneficiaries has widened to encompass the entire entertainment world. Regular benefit performances and the like have been held in its support by the entertainment industry since the 1840s. Its history, *The Royal General Theatrical Fund 1838-1988* by Wendy Trewin was published in 1989.

Actors have regularly fallen on hard times and this benevolent fund has often been able to help. The Fund holds records, minute books, appeal letters and responses since its inception and it may be able to aid family historians if full details about an ancestor can be supplied. In the first instance enquirers should write to the Secretary of the Fund at 11 Garrick Street, London, WC2E 9AR (admin@trtf.com) giving as much detail as they can. In particular stage names are important because some records are maintained under this heading. A query will require research by the Fund's staff which can only be carried out if time permits. It is for this reason that requests for information should always be made in writing.

There are other benevolent funds which cover the entertainment industry, some of which could be of use to the family historian. Among the oldest is the Actor's Benevolent Fund, founded in 1882. The funds are all listed on the Entertainment Charities Guide (www.tactactors.org) on the world wide web.

British Music Hall Society

Contact with this Society is via its website (www.music-hall-society.com) and its archivist. The Society has its own holdings of original music hall material and its officers have been found by enquirers to be helpful and understanding of the needs and interests of family historians. The Society holds regular study groups on the history of the music hall, and the website links with other societies committed to the celebration of music hall in its various forms. A quarterly magazine is published entitled *The Call Boy*.

Music hall performances are also staged on a regular basis chiefly in London. The Society has a committed membership and it should be remembered when contacting the officers that they are volunteers and there are no professional staff. Response times may therefore vary.

Trade Unions

Equity is the trades union covering the entertainment industry which was formed in 1930 by a group of London West End theatre performers. The main office is at Guild House, Upper St. Martins Lane, London, WC2H 9EG (www.equity.org.uk) with regional offices. They maintain membership records. The Musicians Union 60-62 Clapham Road, London, SW9 0JJ (www.musiciansunion.org.uk) seeks to improve the status and conditions of its members. It has archives of its committees' minutes from the late 19th century onwards and membership records from 1930.

Sound archives

If your ancestor worked in the twentieth century, it could be that a recording of their voice has been kept. There are extensive collections and indexes at the National Sound Archive located at the British Library which also includes much of the BBC Sound Archive (www.bl.uk). There are 2.5 million recordings in the sound archive, and from the web page it is even possible to hear many of them at home on a computer. There are also individual recorded interviews. For example the Vicinus Music Hall collection has 71 cassettes of individual interviews recorded during 1974/75 period. The BBC Written Archives located at Caversham Park, Reading, RG4 8TZ (www.bbc.co.uk/heritage/research) has extensive records of correspondence, contracts and much else involving entertainers of all kinds.

Picture Libraries

When researches have shown who your ancestor was and where he or she performed, a next step is to obtain a drawing or photograph of them. This may not be possible for the most obscure figures of course but for those who had even a short period in the limelight as an entertainer then an engraving or photograph may well be found. Most repositories have photos of local entertainment figures but locating the one you want can be a real problem.

The picture libraries operate commercially by providing information from their indexes and reproductions of an original image. Their fees and charges can vary significantly. A list of picture libraries and photographers can be found in Part 4 of the *Directory of Performing Arts Resources* - for details see the introduction to the List of Repositories section.

The larger and most well known collections are:

The Hulton Getty Picture Collection 101 Bayham Street London NWI 0AG. 020 7267 8988 (www.getty-images.com) is possibly the largest and most comprehensive picture library in the world. Its collections cover from the earliest days of photography and before to the present. It's obviously very strong on the whole range of entertainment during the twentieth century, but it also has collections covering the Victorian and Edwardian circus, stage and music hall performers and performances as well as related ephemera including postcards and playbills.

Illustrated London News Picture Library 20 Upper Ground, London SE1 9PF. 020 7805 5585 (www.Ilnpictures.co.uk) has images and content for reproduction from the *Illustrated London News*, known for its engravings from its earliest issues in 1842, and for runs of the *Illustrated Sporting & Dramatic News* and numerous other journals, chiefly twentieth century, which include photographs and drawings of entertainment figures. The Library is digitising its material. Elaine Hart has described the Library in the *Genealogists' Magazine*, Sept 2000, Vol 26 No 11.

Museum of London Picture Library London Wall, London. EC2Y 5HN. 020 7814 5604 www.museumoflondon.org.uk possesses a large collection of images of London life dating from many hundreds of years ago to the present. It has a selection of paintings, prints, drawings and photographs of London places of entertainment from the eighteenth century onwards. The Library has prints and photographs of several famous actors and actresses both on-stage and off, together with their costumes and other ephemera, including posters, playbills and programmes.

For those with a connection to the famous, the National Portrait Gallery Archive (www.npg.org.uk) could well be able to help locate a picture in their collection.

ENSA and CEMA

ENSA (Entertainments National Services Association) was formed in 1938 to provide entertainment for British and allied forces throughout the world during the Second World War. Operating from Drury Lane from 1940 it worked through the NAAFI, which dealt with the financial aspects. ENSA provided a touring programme of entertainment of every type, not only in camps and hostels in Britain but on all war fronts. It employed actors and entertainers of various types including serving members of the armed forces. The organisation ceased after the conclusion of war. Family historians with relations who may have served in ENSA should always attempt to locate them through the usual channels for armed services personnel. Specific ENSA related records are few; some are located at the Imperial War Museum in London (www.iwm.org.uk).

CEMA (Council for the Encouragement of Music and the Arts) was founded in Britain in 1940 to provide entertainment in factories and evacuation camps throughout the country. It took entertainment into unprofitable areas in war time. In 1946 it changed into the Arts Council of Great Britain. It's understood that the Arts Council does not hold records dating from this period which will directly aid the family historian.

LIST OF REPOSITORIES

This listing has been created from a variety of sources which includes the *Directory of Performing Arts Resources*, compiled by Francesca Franchi, Society for Theatre Research, Third Edition, 1998 (in association with the Theatre Museum, London); the SIBMAS International Directory of Performing Arts Collections and Institutions (cf. website below); Backstage (cf. website below); *British Archives, A Guide to Archive Resources in the UK*, Macmillan, London; and the *Family and Local History Handbook*, latest edition. Even so the list cannot be considered exhaustive.

Some of the collections mentioned have indexes to their holdings but the majority do not. Existing indexes are not listed as they are in a constant state of development; it's essential to enquire about the latest position on finding aids. Telephone numbers, website and e-mail addresses can change over time so their correctness cannot be guaranteed; consulting the SIBMAS Directory, mentioned below, or the latest version of a family history directory is recommended. Family historians looking for theatre ancestors will find their usual path to the County Record Offices and Local Studies Collections will remain essentially the same. London is pre-eminent when researching the theatre on a national basis; there is almost too much in the many repositories. Collections only holding material on theatre buildings and construction have not been included, nor those involved only with music and ballet. Some of the institutions on this list require written application before a visit can be made, many more require advance notice.

The following are the specialist sources to be consulted for more detailed information:

Directory of Performing Arts Resources. ISBN 0 85430 0635 price £18 and can be obtained from the Theatre Museum, London. The third edition builds on the second edition published in 1986, and was based on questionnaires as well as other sources including SIBMAS. For those wanting to work from a published source this book is an essential tool. The book is no longer up-to-date in this fast-changing field so has be to be supplemented from other sources.

International Directory of Performing Arts Collections and Institutions (SIBMAS) lists over 7000 international institutions with material relating to the performing arts (theatre, opera, music, ballet, film, circus, radio, television, cabaret, pantomime). Not only basic information about the institution is provided, but also information about collections held by the institution. This massive website (www.theatrelibrary.org/sibmas/idpac/) lists the overwhelming majority of organisations that the family historian will need to consult. An entry on the SIBMAS site typically gives the following information on an institution: address, phone number, e-mail, website, databases held, times of opening, subjects covered, make-up of material, list of performing arts special collections and archive material collections on individuals. The emphasis is on collections of archive material and related books.

Backstage is a web-based national performing arts facility (www.backstage.ac.uk) which seeks to provide a single point of entry for finding and researching collections related to stage and theatre history in the UK. It started with collections contained in certain universities and institutions participating in the original scheme (the Bodleian Library, Royal Holloway College London, University College Northampton and the Universities of Birmingham, Bristol, Exeter, Hull and Kent) but is being extended to take in many more repositories. The long term aim is to produce an online version of the *Directory of Performing Arts Resources*. This is an ambitious project and not likely to see early completion. From the material at present on Backstage, it is possible to search for a specific name and obtain a list of references when, for example, it appears on nineteenth century playbills contained within the collections.

www.applausesw.org.uk is a web-based listing which gives detailed information on holdings by repositories of original material held on theatres in the West of England, including Bath, Bristol, Plymouth and Exeter plus others in smaller towns. The database also gives detail on the main figures associated with the theatre in question, as well as images and details of histories of the theatre or hall in a particular location and the dates of its existence.

THE COLLECTIONS

Abbreviations: CL - Central Library, LSD - Local Studies Department or Collection, CRO - County Record Office, PL - Public Library, RL - Reference Library, RO - Record Office, TR - Theatre Royal

ABERDEEN CL LSD, Rosemount Viaduct, Aberdeen, Grampian, AB25 1GW.
01224 62511. e-mail refloc@artsrec.aberdeen.net.uk
Substantial collection on the theatrical history of Aberdeen, 19th century onwards.

ABERDEEN UNIVERSITY, Heritage Division, Special Collections and Archives, King's College, Aberdeen, Grampian, AB24 3SW. e-mail speclib@abdn.ac.uk
www.abdn.ac.uk/diss/heritage
Archives relating to theatre companies, texts of plays, posters and local newspapers from 1748.

ABERYSTYWYTH, National Library of Wales, Ceredigion, Aberystwyth, Dyfed, SY23 3BU. 01970 623816. e-mail holi@llgc.org.uk www.llgc.org.uk
Extensive collection of items relating to the theatre in Wales, in Welsh and England. In addition it is a British copyright library.

ALDEBURGH, The Britten-Pears Library, The Red House, Aldeburgh, Suffolk, IP15 5PZ. www.lib.uea.ac.uk.
Besides material on Benjamin Britten contains material on British 20th century opera.

ANGUS Archives Service, 214 High Street, Montrose, Tayside, DD10 8HF. 01674 673256. e-mail angu.archives@angus.gov.uk www.angus.gov.uk/history
Archives and cuttings of 20th century local entertainers and theatre.

AYLESBURY Buckinghamshire RO, County Hall, Walton Street, Aylesbury, HP20 1UU. 01296 382587. e-mail archives@buckscc.gov.uk
www.buckscc.gov.uk/leisure/libraries/archives
Records associated with local theatres, 19th & 20th century.

BARNSTAPLE North Devon RO, Tuly Street, Barnstaple, Devon, EX31 1EL. 01271 388608. e-mail ndevrec@devon-cc.gov.uk www.devon.cc.gov.uk/dro/homepage
Records associated with local theatres and amateur productions, 19th & 20th centuries.

BATH CL, 19 The Podium, Northgate Street, Bath, Somerset, BA1 5AN. 01225 787400/428144. e-mail bathlibraries@bathnes.gov.uk
Large collection of varied material relating to TR Bath, 18th century onwards.

BEAMISH, The North of England Open Air Museum Archives, Beamish, County Durham. DH9 ORG. 0191 370 4016. www.beamish.org.uk
Theatre posters etc. relating to the North East of England.

BEDFORD CRO, County Hall, Cauldwell Street, Bedford, MK42 9AP. 01234 228833. e-mail archive@csd.bedfordshire.gov.uk www.bedfordshire.gov.uk
Archive material relating to Bedfordshire theatres,17th century onwards.

BEDFORD Museum, Castle Lane, Bedford, MK40 3XD. 01234 353323. e-mail bmuseum@bedford.gov.uk www.bedfordmuseum.org.uk
A few 18th & 19th century local playbills.

BELFAST Lyric Theatre Archive - at present housed at the Linen Hall Library Belfast (see below)
Extensive theatre material from the theatre and associated groups.

BELFAST Public Record Office of Northern Ireland, 66 Balmoral Avenue, Belfast, Northern Ireland, BT9 6NY. 028 9025 5905. e-mail proni@nics.gov.uk
www.proni.nics.gov.uk
A range of theatrical material relating to Ireland.

BELFAST The Linen Hall Library, 17 Donegall Square North, Belfast, Northern Ireland, BT1 5GD. 028 9043 8586. e-mail info@linenhall.com www.linenhall.com
Collection of theatre material relating to 20th century theatre in Ulster.

BIRKENHEAD Wirral Archives Service, Birkenhead Town Hall, Hamilton Street, Birkenhead, Merseyside, L41 5BR. 0151 666 4010.
e-mail archives@wirral-libraries.net
Material related to the Argyle Theatre of Varieties, Birkenhead 1867-1940.

BIRMINGHAM CL, Arts Languages and Literature Service, Chamberlain Square, Birmingham, West Midlands, B3 3HQ. 0121 235 4229.
e-mail archives@birmingham.gov.uk www.birmingham.gov.uk/libraries/archives/home
Extensive records relating to Birmingham and London theatres, 17th century onwards. A major Shakespeare collection.

BIRMINGHAM LSD and City Archives, CL, Chamberlain Square, Birmingham, West Midlands, B3 3HQ. 0121 303 4217. e-mail archives@birmingham.gov.uk
www.birmingham.gov.uk/libraries/archives/home
Programmes etc. for over sixty professional and amateur theatres in Birmingham, including the Birmingham Repertory Theatre and TR, and theatres and companies in the area including the Black Country, both amateur and professional, 18th century onwards.

BIRMINGHAM University Library, Special Collections Department, Edgbaston, Birmingham, West Midlands, B15 2TT. 0121 414 5839. www.bham.ac.uk/olrc/index
Theatre collection relating to performance at theatres in London, Birmingham and Stratford, 18th century onwards.

BLACKBURN CL, Town Hall Street, Blackburn, Lancashire, BB2 1AG. 01254 587920. e-mail reference.library@blackburn.gov.uk
Local playbills etc. and cuttings, from 18th century.

BOURNEMOUTH RL, Meyrick Road, Bournemouth, Dorset, BH1 3DJ. 01202
292021. e-mail enquiries@bournemouth.gov.uk
Programmes, playbills etc. for Bournemouth theatres, 19th & 20th centuries.

BOURNEMOUTH Russell-Cotes Museum, East Cliff, Bournemouth, Dorset, BH1
3AA. 01202 451800. www.russell-coates.bournemouth.gov.uk
London theatre material mainly relating to Sir Henry Irving and Lyceum Theatre, plus
non-British items.

BRADFORD Bolling Hall Museum, Bowling Hall Road, Bradford, West Yorkshire,
BD4 7LP. 01274 723057. www.bradford.gov.uk/museums/bolling
Playbills and programmes relating to Bradford theatres.

BRADFORD West Yorkshire Archives Service, Bradford District Archives, 15 Canal
Street, Bradford, West Yorkshire, BD1 4AT. 01274 731931.
e-mail bradford@wyasbrad.org.uk www.archives.wyjs.org.uk
Extensive archives relating to Bradford & Halifax theatres, 19th & 20th centuries.

BRIGHTON LSD, Church Street, Brighton, East Sussex, BN1 1UD. 01273 296971
e-mail brightonlibrary@pavillion.co.uk
Large collection of playbills and programmes for Brighton theatres and the Bloomfield
collection of London theatre playbills, 19th & 20th centuries.

BRIGHTON Royal Pavilion Art Gallery & Museum, 4-5 Pavilion Buildings, Brighton,
East Sussex, BN1 1UE. 01273 290900. www.brighton.virtualmuseum/info
Theatre programmes etc. for Brighton theatres, 19th & 20th centuries.

BRIGHTON University of Sussex Manuscript Section, Falmer, Brighton, East Sussex,
BN1 9QL. 01273 678157. www.susx.ac.uk
Manuscripts relating to certain well known theatre figures.

BRISTOL Old Vic Company, Theatre Royal, King Street, Bristol, BS1 4ED.
0117 949 3993. www.bristol-old-vic.co.uk
TR and Bristol Old Vic archives but most historical records are in Bristol City Record
Office.

BRISTOL RO, B Bond Warehouse, Smeaton Road, Bristol, BS1 6XN. 0117 922 4224.
e-mail bro@bristol-city.gov.uk
Extensive records relating to Bristol theatres, as well as other theatres in South East
England and London.

BRISTOL RL, College Green, Bristol, BS1 5TL. 0117 903 7200.
e-mail bristol_library_service@bristol-city.gov.uk
Substantial collection of programmes etc. of Bristol theatres, with index to the playbills.

BRISTOL University Theatre Collection. Department of Drama, Canticks Close,
Bristol, BS8 1UP. 0117 928 7836. e-mail theatre-collection@bris.ac.uk
www.bris.ac.uk/theatrecollection
An extensive collection of West Country playbills etc. and theatre ephemera (Eric Jones-
Evans collection), plus the Beerbohm Tree collection and the London Old Vic archive.

BROMLEY CL LSD, High Street, Bromley, Kent, BR1 1EX. 020 8460 9955.
e-mail reference.library@bromley.gov.uk
Programmes etc. for Bromley & Penge theatres, and the extensive Crystal Palace
Collection 1854-1936.

BURNLEY CL LSD, Grimshaw Street, Burnley, Lancashire, BB11 2BD.
01282 437115. e-mail burnley.reference@lcl.lancscc.gov.uk
Programmes etc. for theatres in the Burnley area, both professional & amateur.

BURNLEY Towneley Hall Museums, Burnley, Lancashire, BB11 3RQ.
01282 424213. www.bunley.gov.uk/towneley
Playbills etc. relating to Burnley theatres, 19th & 20th centuries.

BURY CL LSD, Manchester Road, Bury, Lancashire BL9 0DG. 0161 253 5871.
e-mail information@bury.gov.uk www.bury.gov.uk/culture
Records relating to theatres in Bury, including TR and Hippodrome.

BUXTON Museum, Terrace Road, Buxton, Derbyshire, SK17 6DU. 01298 24658.
e-mail buxton.museum@derbyshire.gov.uk www.buxton.museum.derbyshire.gov.uk
Playbills etc. from 1790s relating to Buxton theatres and Festival.

CAERNARFON RO, Victoria Dock, Caernarfon, Gwynedd, North Wales, LL55 1SH.
01286 679095. e-mail archifau@gwynedd.gov.uk
www.gwynedd.gov.uk/adrannau/addysg/archifau
Playbills, programmes etc. for theatrical performances in the North Wales area.

CAMBRIDGE CL LSD, 7 Lion Yard, Cambridge, CB2 3QD. 01223 712008.
e-mail cambridge.central.library@cambridgeshire.gov.uk
Playbills and records relating to Cambridge and area theatres from 18th century
onwards.

CAMBRIDGE CRO, Shire Hall, Castle Hill, Cambridge, CB3 0AP. 01223 717281.
e-mail county.records.cambridge@camcty.gov.uk
www.cambridgeshire.gov.uk/sub/archive
Miscellaneous records relating to Cambridgeshire theatres.

CAMBRIDGE University Library, West Road, Cambridge, CB3 9DR. 01223 333000.
e-mail library@lib.com.ac.uk www.lib.cam.ac.uk
Large collection of 20th century Cambridge theatre programmes. It is a British copyright
library.

CAMBRIDGE Modern Archive Centre, King's College, Cambridge, CB2 1ST.
01223 331444. e-mail librarian@kings.cam.ac.uk www. bear.kings.ac.uk/library
Miscellaneous papers including ballet, and of the Cambridge Arts Theatre.

CANTERBURY City & Cathedral Archives, The Precincts, Canterbury, Kent,
CT1 2EH. 01227 463510. e-mail archives@canterbury-cathedral.org
www.canterbury-cathedral.org
Miscellaneous theatre collection including the James Miller music hall collection.

CANTERBURY Library LSD, High Street, Canterbury, Kent, CT1 2JF.
01227 463608. e-mail canterbury.library@kent.gov.uk
www.librarycircle.cant.ac.uk/infopages/cantpublic
Playbills, programmes etc. for Canterbury theatres including the TR.

CANTERBURY Royal City Museum, Canterbury, Kent, CT1 2RA. 01227 452747.
e-mail museums@canterbury.gov.uk
Gordon collection of playbills.

CANTERBURY University of Kent, Templeman Library Special Collections,
Canterbury, Kent, CT2 7NX. 01277 823570. e-mail library@ukc.ac.uk
www.ukc.ac.uk/library
Extensive collection of theatre records, including music hall. See indexes on
www.backstage.ac.uk/index_html

CARDIFF Welsh National Opera Archives, John Street, Cardiff, South Glamorgan,
CF1 4SP. 01222 464666.
Material on Welsh National Opera's history.

CARLISLE Cumbria CRO, The Castle, Carlisle, CA3 8UR. 01228 607285. e-mail
carlisle.recordoffice@cumbriacc.gov.uk www. cumbria.gov.uk/archives/
Collection of material on Carlisle theatres and performances, 17th century onwards.

CHELMSFORD Essex CRO, Wharf Road, Chelmsford, CM2 6YT. 01245 244644.
e-mail ero.enquiry@essexcc.gov.uk www.essexcc.gov.uk
Sources and original material on Essex theatre history.

CHELTENHAM Museum & LSD, Clarence Street, Cheltenham, Gloucestershire,
GL50 3JT. 01242 532688. e-mail artgallery@cheltenham.gov.uk
Theatre playbills from the 1790's for Cheltenham theatres and other Gloucestershire
towns.

CHESHIRE & CHESTER Archives & LSD, Duke Street, Chester, Cheshire,
CH1 1RL. 01244 602574. e-mail recordoffice@cheshire.gov.uk
www.cheshire.gov.uk/recoff/home
Theatre licensing records etc. for Cheshire. Programmes etc. relating to Chester theatres,
chiefly 20th century.

CHESTERFIELD CL LSD, New Beetwell Street, Chesterfield, Derbyshire, S40 1QN.
01246 209292. e-mail chesterfield.library@derbyshire.gov.uk
Programmes etc. relating to Chesterfield theatres, chiefly 20th century.

CHICHESTER West Sussex RO, County Hall, Chichester, West Sussex, PO19 1RN.
01243 533911. e-mail records.office@westsussex.gov.uk www.west
sussex.gov.uk/cs/ro/rohome
Playbills etc. for West Sussex theatres, with emphasis on those in Chichester, 18th
century onwards.

COLCHESTER Museums Resource Centre, 14 Ryegate Road, Colchester, Essex,
CO1 1YG. 01206 282935. www.colchestermuseums.org.uk
A limited number of 19th century playbills relating to Colchester.

COLNE Library, Market Street, Colne, Lancashire, BB8 OAP. 01282 871155.
e-mail colne.reference@lcl.lancscc.gov.uk
Limited number of theatrical items relating to Colne.

COSELEY Dudley Archives & LSD, Mount Pleasant Street, Coseley, West Midlands,
WV14 9JR. 01384 812770. e-mail archives.pls@mbc.dudley.gov.uk
www.dudley.gov.uk/council/library /archives.htm
Records and programmes relating to Dudley and Stourbridge theatres, 19th & 20th
centuries.

COVENTRY CL, Coventry & Warwickshire Collection, Smithfield Way, Coventry, West Midlands, CV1 1FY. 01203 832336. e-mail covinfo@discover. co.uk
www.coventry.org.uk/accent
Playbills, programmes etc. for Coventry theatres mainly 19th & 20th centuries.

CROYDON PL, LSD, Katherine Street, Croydon, Surrey, CR9 1ET. 020 8760 5400. e-mail local studies@library.croydon.gov.uk www.croydon.gov.uk/cr-libls
Programmes, posters etc. for numerous Croydon and area theatres.

CWMBRAN Gwent CRO, County Hall, Cwmbran, Gwent, NP44 2XH. 01633 644886. e-mail 113057.2173@compuserve.com
Material mainly relating to the Hendre Theatre.

DARLINGTON Borough of Darlington Museum, Tubwell Row, Darlington, Durham, DL1 1PD. 01325 463795. www.darlington.gov.uk
Limited number of playbills, programmes relating to Darlington theatres.

DARLINGTON Darlington Library LSD, Crown Street, Darlington, Durham, DL1 1ND. 01325 462034/349630. e-mail crown.street.library@darlington.gov.uk
Posters, playbills, programmes etc. relating to Darlington theatres, 19th & 20th centuries.

DERBY LSD, 25b, Irongate, Derby, Derbyshire, DE1 3GL. 01332 255393.
e-mail local studies.library@derby.gov.uk
Playbills, programmes covering Derby and some Derbyshire theatres 19th & 20th centuries.

DONCASTER Archives Department, King Edward Road, Doncaster, South Yorkshire, DN4 ONA, 01302 859811 e-mail doncasterarchives@hotmail.com
www.doncaster.gov.uk/education/ document
Various items relating to Doncaster theatres, both professional and amateur.

DONCASTER LSD, CL,Waterdale, Doncaster, South Yorkshire, DN1 3JE.
01302 734307. e-mail reference.library@doncaster.gov.uk
Playbills and other records relating to Doncaster theatres, from 18th century onwards.

DORCHESTER RL, Colliton Park, Dorchester, Dorset, DT1 1XJ. 01305 224448.
e-mail dorchesterreflibrary@dorsetcc.gov.uk www.dorsetcc.gov.uk/libraries
Programmes etc. for Dorchester and Weymouth theatres from the 18th century onwards.
Thomas Hardy collection of material relating to the performance of his plays.

DORCHESTER Archives Service, Bridport Road, Dorchester, Dorset, DT1 1RP.
01305 250550. www.dorsetcc.gov.uk
Collection of playbills, programmes etc. from Dorset theatres.

DORCHESTER Natural History & Archaelogical Society Library, Dorset County
Museum, High West Street, Dorchester, Dorset, DT1 1XA. 01305 262735.
Programmes and posters of performances in 19th century Dorset theatres, and of
performances of the novels of Thomas Hardy.

DUNDEE City Council CL, The Wellgate, Dundee, DD1 1DB. 01382 434377.
e-mail local.studies@dundeecity.gov.uk www.dundeecity.gov.uk/dcchtml/nrd/centlib/
Mainly works on early music, but the Lamb Collection of ephemera has performing arts
material from the 19th century, mainly for Dundee.

DURHAM CRO, County Hall, Durham, DH1 5UL. 0191 3833474.
e-mail recordooffice@durham.gov.uk www.durham.gov.uk/recordoffice
Collections of playbills, programmes etc. for County of Durham theatres, 19th century
onwards.

DURHAM University, Palace Green Section Library, Palace Green, Durham,
DH1 3RN. e-mail PG.Library@durham.ac.uk
Small collection of playbills from Durham theatres, 18th & 19th centuries.

EDINBURGH CL, George IV Bridge, Edinburgh, EH1 1EG. 0131 242 8030.
e-mail eclis@edinburgh.gov.uk www.edinburgh.gov.uk
Extensive collection of playbills, programmes etc. for Edinburgh theatres, 18th century
onwards.

EDINBURGH National Library of Scotland, George IV Bridge, Edinburgh, EH1 1EW.
e-mail enquiries@nls.uk www.nls.uk
Large collection of Edinburgh playbills plus many for London and other theatres. The
theatrical material here and at the central library has been indexed.

EXETER Devon RO, Castle Street, Exeter, Devon, EX4 3PU. 01392 384253.
e-mail devrec@devon-cc.gov.uk www.devon-cc.gov.uk/dro/homepage
Programmes etc. for Exeter and Devon theatres, 19th & 20th centuries.

EXETER Northcott Theatre Archive, Stocker Road, Exeter, Devon, EX4 4QB.
01392 256182. www.applausesw.org.uk/database - for information on holdings of
theatre material in the west of England. Archives of the Northcott Theatre, Exeter
(modern).

EXETER West Country Studies Library, Castle Street, Exeter, Devon, EX4 3PQ.
01392 384216. e-mail dlaw@devon.cc.gov.uk www.devon.cc.gov.uk
Playbills, programmes for Devon theatres, 18th century onwards, professional and amateur. Also the Performing Arts Library at the same address has books on the theatre.

GATESHEAD CL, Prince Consort Road, Gateshead, Tyne & Wear, NE8 4LN.
0191 4773478. e-mail gateslib.demon.co.uk. www.ris.niaa.org.uk.
Small collection of playbills and programmes.

GLASGOW University Library, Scottish Theatre Archive, Hillhead Street, Glasgow,
Strathclyde, G12 8QE. 0141 3306758. www.lib.gla.ac.uk
Extensive holdings of original material on Scottish theatres.

GLASGOW University Library, Special Collections Department, Hillhead Street,
Glasgow, Strathclyde, G12 8QE. 0141 3306797.
e-mail library@uk.ac.glasgow www.gla.ac.uk/library/
A considerable collection of Scottish theatre material including ephemera.

GLASGOW Mitchell Library, Glasgow Room, North Street, Glasgow, Strathclyde,
G3 7DN. 0141 227 2935. e-mail history and glasgow@gls.glasgow.gov.uk
www.libarch.glasgow
Very extensive collection of playbills, programmes etc. covering Glasgow theatres from 18th century onwards. See *Glasgow Theatres & Music Halls: a guide*, 1980.

GLASGOW People's Palace Museum, Glasgow Green, Glasgow, Strathclyde,
G40 1AT. 0141 554 0223. www.clyde-valley.com/glasgow/peoples
Miscellaneous collection of items mainly relating to music hall and vaudeville in the Glasgow area, 19th & 20th centuries.

GLOUCESTER Library, Brunswick Road, Gloucester, Gloucestershire, GL1 1HT.
01452 426979. e-mail clamsgloscc.gov.uk www.gloscc.gov.uk
Miscellaneous theatre material scattered through the County Local History Collections.

GLOUCESTER Gloucestershire CRO, Clarence Row, Alvin Street, Gloucester,
GL1 3DW. 01452 425295. e-mail records@gloscc.gov.uk
www.glosec.gov.uk/pubserv/gcc/corpserve/archives
Varied material covering Gloucestershire theatres, from 18th century onwards.

GRIMSBY RL, Town Hall Square, Grimsby, Lincolnshire, DN31 1HG. 01472 323600.
e-mail librariesandmuseums@nelincs.gov.uk www.nelinks.gov.uk
Miscellaneous items relating to Grimsby theatres, including TR.

HARROGATE North Yorkshire County RL, Victoria Avenue, Harrogate, North Yorkshire, HG1 1EG. 01423 720320. e-mail harrogate.library@northyorks.gov.uk Playbills, programmes etc. for Harrogate theatres, mainly 20th century.

HARTLEPOOL Museum Service, Sir William Gray House, Clarence Road, Hartlepool, Cleveland, TS24 8BT. 01429 523443. www.thisishartlepool.co.uk Theatrical material covering Hartlepool, Stockton and area, 19th century onwards.

HAWARDEN Flintshire CRO, The Old Rectory, Hawarden, Deeside, CH5 3NR. 01244 532364. e-mail archives@flintshire.gov.uk www.flintshire.gov.uk Material related to theatres in Flintshire, professional and amateur, 19th century onwards.

HEREFORD Library LSD, Broad Street, Hereford, Herefordshire, HR4 9AU. 01432 272456. www.libraries.herefordshire.gov.uk Material on history of theatre in the county, including playbills, programmes etc.

HERTFORD Archives & LSD, County Hall, Hertford, Hertfordshire, SG13 8EJ. 01992 555105. e-mail hals@hertscc.gov.uk www.hertsdirect.org Material on Hertford theatres and Welwyn. George Bernard Shaw collection.

HORNCHURCH Library, 44 North Street, Hornchurch, Essex, RM11 1SH. 0170 852248. e-mail info@havering.gov.uk www.havering.gov.uk Comprehensive collection of material on Queen's Theatre Hornchurch, opened in 1953. Detailed index available.

HUDDERSFIELD Tolson Memorial Museum, Ravensknowle Park, Huddersfield, West Yorkshire, HD5 8DJ. 01484 223830. www. kirkleesmc.gov.uk/community/museums/mus Limited number of playbills and programmes on local theatres, mainly 19th century.

HUDDERSFIELD West Yorkshire Archives Service, Kirkless, CL, Princess Alexandra Walk, Huddersfield, HD1 2SU. 01484 221966. e-mail kirklees@wyjs.org.uk www.archives.wyjs.org.uk Material on theatres in the area, both amateur and professional, 19th century onwards.

HULL - see Kingston Upon Hull

HUNTINGDON CRO, Grammar School Walk, Huntingdon, Cambridgeshire, PE18 6LF. 01480 375842. e-mail county.records.hunts@camcnty.gov.uk www.camcnty.gov.uk/sub/archive/huntoff. Material on theatres in area but mainly Huntingdon, 19th century onwards.

INVERNESS Library, Highland County Archive, Farraline Park, Inverness, Highlands, IV1 1NH. 01463 236463. e-mail inverness.library@highland.gov.uk
Playbills for theatres in Inverness, Dingwell and Beauly 1842-51.

IPSWICH Suffolk CRO, Gatacre Road, Ipswich, IP1 2LQ. 01473 584541.
e-mail ipswich.ro@libher.suffolkcc.gov.uk
www.suffolkcc.gov.uk/Libraries_and_heritage/sro/
Records relating to theatres in eastern part of Suffolk, amateur and professional, mainly 20th century.

KING'S LYNN The Lynn Museum, Old Market Street, King's Lynn, Norfolk, PE30 1NL. 01553 775001.www.west-norfolk.gov.uk/westnorfolk/leisure
Poster collection for local theatres, from 18th century onwards.

KINGSTON UPON HULL University of Hull Brynmor Jones Library, Cottingham Road, Kingston upon Hull, Humberside, HU6 7RX. 01482 465265.
e-mail archives@lib.hull.ac.uk www.hull.acc.uk
Playbills, programmes etc. for Hull theatres, and archive records for TR at York, Leeds, Doncaster and Wakefield, 18th century onwards. Indexes available.

KINGSTON UPON HULL Wilberforce House, 25 High Street, Kingston upon Hull, Humberside, HU1 1NQ 01482 613902. www.hullcc.gov.uk/museums/wilberforce/index
Playbills, programmes etc. for TR and other Hull theatres, as well as others in the locality, 18th century onwards. Card index available.

KINGSTON UPON THAMES Kingston Museum & Heritage Service, North Kingston Centre, Richmond Road, Kingston upon Thames, Surrey, KT2 5PE. 020 8547 6738.
e-mail local.history@rbk.kingston.gov.uk www.kingston.gov.uk/museum
Complete set of playbills for the Royal County Theatre also cuttings, plus similar material for the Kingston Empire.

LANCASTER LSD, Divisional Library, Market Square, Lancaster, Lancashire, LA1 1HY. 01524 580700. e-mail library@lcl.lancscc.gv.uk
Playbills, programmes etc. for Lancaster theatres, 18th century onwards.

LEEDS Abbey House Museum, Kirkstall, Leeds, West Yorkshire, LS5 3EH.
0113 2755821 www.leeds.gov.uk/abbeyhouse
Playbills, programmes etc. for Leeds theatres, 19th century onwards.

LEEDS LSD, CL, Calverley Street, Leeds, West Yorkshire, LS1 3AB. 0113 2478290.
e-mail local.studies@leeds.gov.uk www.leeds.gov.uk/library/services/loc reso.
Playbills, programmes for Leeds theatres. Part indexed.

LEEDS University Library, Leeds, West Yorkshire, LS2 9JT. 0113 2431751.
e-mail library@leeds.ac.uk www. leeds.ac.uk/library/
Collection of playbills, programmes etc. for Leeds theatres, plus material on theatres
elsewhere including London, 18th century onwards.

LEEDS West Yorkshire Archives Service, Chapeltown Road, Sheepscar, Leeds, LS6 2AU.
0113 214 5814. e-mail leeds@wyashq.demon.co.uk www.archives.wyjs.org.uk
Playbills, programmes, records etc. for various Leeds theatres, 19th century onwards.
Index and database.

LEICESTER Leicestershire CRO, Long Street, Wigston Magna, Leicester,
Leicestershire, LE18 2AH. 0116 2571080. e-mail recordoffice@leics.gov.uk
Playbills, programmes for Leicester, including TR, and county theatres, 19th century
onwards.

LEIGH Wigan Archives Service, Town Hall, Leigh, Lancashire, WN7 2DY.
01942 404430. e-mail heritage@wiganmbc.gov.uk www.wiganmbc.gov.uk
Theatre material for Wigan area, 19th century onwards.

LEWES East Sussex CRO, The Maltings, Castle Precincts, Lewes, BN7 1NT.
01273 482349. e-mail archives@eastsussexcc.gov.uk www.eastsussex.gov.uk/archives
Theatre material for East Sussex Theatres, 18th century onwards.

LEWES Glyndebourne, Lewes, East Sussex, BN8 5UU. 01273 812321.
www.glyndebourne.com
Documentation covering the history of the Glyndebourne Festival Opera from 1934.

LINCOLN CL LSD, Free School Lane, Lincoln, Lincolnshire, LN2 1EZ.
01522 510800. e-mail lincoln.library@dial.pipex.com
Playbills etc. for Lincolnshire theatres, mainly TR Lincoln, 18th century onwards.

LINCOLN Lincolnshire Archives, St Rumbold Street, Lincoln, Lincolnshire,
LN2 5AB. 01522 526204 e-mail archives@lincolnshire.gov.uk
www.lincs-archives.com
Playbills, programmes for Lincolnshire theatres, 18th century onwards.

LIVERPOOL Public Library RO & LSD, William Brown Street, Liverpool, Merseyside, L3 8EW. 0151 233 5417. e-mail recoffice.central.library@liverpool.gov.uk www.liverpool.gov.uk
Extensive collection of playbills, programmes etc. for Liverpool theatres, 18th century onwards. The Public Library has a large stock of books on the theatre.

LONDON, Barnet Libraries, LSD, Hendon Library, The Burroughs, Hendon, London, NW4 4BE. 020 8359 2876. e-mail hendon.library@barnet.gov.uk
Programmes etc. for the Golders Green Theatre.

LONDON, British Library, 96 Euston Road, London, NW1 2DB. 020 7412 7000. www.portico.bl.uk
Besides being the major copyright library for books, it hold a very extensive collection of theatre material covering London and provincial theatres, 17th century onwards. In addition it holds the plays submitted to the Lord Chamberlain from 1824 to 1968; there is a published guide to this collection.

LONDON, British Library Newspaper Library, Colindale Avenue, London, NW9 5HE. 020 7412 7533. e-mail newspaper@bl.uk www.bl.uk/collections/newspaper
The chief repository for theatrical newpapers in the UK.

LONDON, British Library of Political & Economic Science, London School of Economics, 10 Portugal Street, London, WC2A 2HD. 020 7955 7223. www.lse.ac.uk/blpes/archives
Leaflets, posters and programmes for gay theatre productions. George Bernard Shaw Business Papers.

LONDON, British Museum, Department of Prints & Drawings, Great Russell Street, London, WC1B 3DG. 020 7323 8408. e-mail archives@thebritishmuseum.ac.uk www.thebritishmuseum.ac.uk
Large collection of portraits of 18th & 19th century leading actors.

LONDON, Bromley PL, 206d Anerley Road, London, SE20 8TJ 020 8778 7457. www.bromley.gov.uk
Material relating to performances at the Crystal Palace.

LONDON, Camden LSD, Holborn Library, 32-38 Theobalds Road, London, WC1X 8PA. 020 7974 6342. www.camden.gov.uk
Collection of material on Camden and Holborn theatres.

LONDON Chelsea LSD, Chelsea Library, Old Town Hall, King's Road, London, SW3 5EZ. 020 7352 6056. www.rbkc.gov.uk/libraries
Collection of material on Chelsea Palace and Royal Court Theatre.

LONDON, Cinema Museum, the Old Fire Station, 46 Renfrew Road, London, SE11 4NA. 0207 820 9991. e-mail cinema.museum@dial.pipex.com
Theatre programmes etc. for London and provincial theatres, 19th century onwards.

LONDON, Cuming Museum, 155-157 Walworth Road, London, SE17 1RS. 020 7701 1342. e-mail cuming.museum@southwark.gov.uk
www.southwark.gov.uk/culture.heritage/cuming
Playbills, programmes etc. and some material on the Tudor theatre.

LONDON, Ealing Library LSD, CL, 103 Ealing Broadway Centre, The Broadway, London, W5 5JY. 020 8567 3656. e-mail localhistory@hotmail.com
Material on the Questors Theatre Ealing, and Bankside Little Theatre.

LONDON, Enfield Libraries, LSD, Southgate Town hall, Green Lanes, London, N13 4XZ. 020 8379 2244. www.enfield.gov.uk.
Playbills, programmes etc., 19th century onwards, professional and amateur theatre.

LONDON, English National Opera Archives, ENO Works, 40 Pitfield Street, London, N1 6EU. 020 7729 9610. www.eno.org
Material relating to Sadler's Wells Opera from 1931, English National Opera and London Coliseum.

LONDON, Finsbury Archive, London Borough of Islington, 245 St John Street, London, EC1V 4NB. 020 7609 3051. www.islington.gov.uk/htm
The Sadlers Wells collection, one of the largest collections in London on an individual theatre, 18th century onwards.

LONDON, Graeme Cruickshank Theatre Collection, The place Theatre, 171 Torridon Road, London, SE6 1RG. 120 8695 5480. e-mail graeme@stagemanagementsociety.co.uk
A private collection of theatre items chiefly covering the Duke of York's and the Barnes Theatre.

LONDON, Greenwich Library LSD, Woodlands, 90 Mycenae Road, Greenwich, London, SE3 7SE. 020 8858 4631. e-mail local.history@greenwich.gov.uk
Playbills, programmes for Greenwich theatres, 18th century onwards.

LONDON, Guildhall Library Print Room, Aldermanbury, London, EX2P 2EJ.
020 7332 1839. e-mail prints.guildhall@ms.corpoflondon.gov.uk
Extensive collection of playbills, programmes, ephemera and prints for London and
provincial theatres, 18th century onwards.

LONDON, Gunnersbury Park Museum, Gunnersbury Park, Popes Lane, London,
W3 8QL. 020 8992 1612. www.gp_museum@cip.org.uk
Small collections of playbills etc. for London theatres, and material relating to the
Chiswick Empire.

LONDON, Hackney Archives Department, 43 De Beauvoir Road, London, N1 5SQ.
020 7241 2886. e-mail archives@hackney.gov.uk www.hackney.gov.uk
Extensive collection of material on Hackney area theatres, including Hackney Empire
and those in Shoreditch and the City of London, 18th century onwards.

LONDON, Hammersmith & Fulham Archives & LSD, The Lilla Huset, 191 Talgarth
Road, London W6 8BJ. 020 8741 5159. www.Ftech.net/-haflibs
Extensive material on local theatres, including Olympia and Earls Court, 18th century
onwards.

LONDON Holborn Library LSD, 32-38 Theobalds Road, London WC1X 8PA.
020 7974 6342. e-mail localstudies@camden.gov.uk www.camden.gov.uk
Collection of material on Holborn, Camden and West end theatres.

LONDON, Imperial War Museum, Department of Documents, Lambeth Road,
London, SE1 6HZ. 020 7416 5344. e-mail books@iwm.org.uk www.iwm.org.uk
Material on entertainment for the forces in war time, with some ENSA material
(Entertainments National Service Association, the organisation which in World War 2
provided concerts and shows for British forces).

LONDON, Islington Libraries LSD, CL, 2 Fieldway Crescent, London, N5 1PF.
020 7619 6931. e-mail local.history@islington.gov.uk www.islington.gov.uk
Playbills, programmes etc. for local theatres including leading music halls, 19th
century onwards.

LONDON, Kensington & Chelsea LSD, CL, Hornton Street, London, W8 7RX.
020 7937 2542. www.rbkc.gov.uk/libraries
A few items on local theatres.

LONDON, Lambeth Libraries and Archives Department, Minet Library, 52 Knatchball Road, London, SE5 9QY. 020 7926 6076. www.lambeth.landmark.com
Large collections of playbills for Lambeth & Surrey theatres, including the Surrey Theatre, Astley's and the Old Vic.

LONDON, Lewisham Libraries LSD, 199-201 Lewisham High Street, London, SE13 6LG. 020 8297 0682. e-mail local studies@lewisham.gov.uk www.lewisham.gov.uk
Material from local theatre both professional and amateur, 19th century onwards.

LONDON, London Metropolitan Archives, 40 Northampton Road, London, EC1R OHB. 020 7332 3520. e-mail ask.lma@ms.corpoflondon.gov.uk
www.corpoflondon.gov.uk/archives/lma
Extensive records relating to London theatres from the 16th century onwards.

LONDON, London Palladium Theatre Archive, Argyll Street, London, W1A 3AB. 020 7437 6166.
Material related to London Palladium and Stoll Moss Theatres.

LONDON, Mander & Mitchenson Theatre Collection, Jerwood Library of the Performing Arts, Trinity School of Music, King Charles Court, Old Royal Naval College, Greenwich, London, SE10 9JF. 020 8305 4426.
www.mander-and-mitchenson.co.uk
An extensive collection on all aspects of the theatre including playbills, programmes, prints etc. Widely used as a source for illustrations. Very strong on London theatres. Phone before attempting to visit.

LONDON, Museum of London, London Wall, London, EC2Y 5HN. 020 7600 1058. e-mail mus@museum-london.org.uk www.museum-london.org.uk
Playbills, programmes, scrapbooks etc. of London theatres, mainly from 18th century onwards.

LONDON, National Film & TV Archive, British Folm Institute, 21 Stephen Street, London, W1P 2LN. 020 7255 1444. www.bfi.org.uk
Entertainment figures on film etc.

LONDON, National Portrait Gallery Archive & Library, St Martin's Place, London, WC2H OHE. 020 7306 0055. www.npg.org.uk
A reference collection of engravings and photographs of theatrical personalities

LONDON, National Theatre Museum, 1E Tavistock Street, London WC2E 7PA.
020 7836 7891. www.vam.ac.uk/thm
A massive collection of theatre material, which systematically collects theatre programmes from over 200 UK theatres. Access by appointment only well in advance.

LONDON, Newham PL LSD, Water Lane, Stratford, London, E15 4NJ.
020 8534 4545. www.newham.gov.uk
Material associated with TR Stratford, and East and West Ham theatres and music halls.

LONDON, Palace Theatre Archive, Shaftesbury Avenue, London, W1V 8AY.
020 7434 0088.
Material related to Palace Theatre and other London theatres and music halls. Index to variety artistes and acts (1892-1914).

LONDON, Playhouse Archive, Northumberland Avenue, London, WC2N 5DE.
020 7839 4292.
Material related to the Avenue Theatre and the Playhouse.

LONDON, Queen Mary & Westfield College Main Library, 327 Mile End Road, London, E1 4NS. 020 7975 5555. www.library.qmv.ac.uk
Playbills, programmes etc. related to the People's Palace. Library to support university courses.

LONDON, Royal Academy of Dramatic Art Library, 18 Chenies Street, London, WC1E 6PA. 020 7908 4878. e-mail library@rada.ac.uk
RADA Archives, record of students from 1904, name only until 1920s. Large collection of press cuttings, books etc. on the theatre.

LONDON, Royal College of Music, Portrait Collection, Prince Consort Road, London, SW7 2BS. 020 7591 4340. www.rcm.ac.uk
Extensive collection of portraits of musicians and performers.

LONDON, Royal National Theatre Archives, Salisbury House, 1-3 Brixton Road, London, SW9 6DE. 020 7820 3512. e-mail archives@nationaltheatre.org.uk
www.nationaltheatre.org.uk/archives
Records associated with the Royal National Theatre since 1963.

LONDON, Royal Opera House Archives, Covent Garden, London, WC2E 9DD.
020 7212 9353. www.roh.org.uk/house
Archives of the Royal Opera House etc. from 1732.

LONDON, Southwark LSD, 211 Borough High Street, London, SE1 1JA. 020 7403 3507. e-mail local.studies.library@southwark.gov.uk www.southwark.gov.uk
Playbills, programmes etc. for Southwark and adjacent area theatres, 17th century onwards.

LONDON, Theatre Royal Drury Lane Archive, Catherine Street, London, WC2B 5JF. 020 7437 6166.
Material relating to the theatre's history and Stoll Moss theatres.

LONDON, Tower Hamlets PL LSD. Bancroft Library, 277 Bancroft Road, London, E1 4DQ. 020 8980 4366. e-mail bancroftlibrary@towerhamlets.gov.uk
Material, mainly press cuttings, on Stepney, Whitechapel and Poplar theatres.

LONDON, University College Library, Gower Street, London, WC1E 6BT. 020 7380 7796. www.ucl.ac.uk/special-col
Material relating to the Bloomsbury Theatre and Student Drama Society, 1920s to date.

LONDON, University of North London Learning Centre, 236 Holloway Road, London, N7 6PP. 020 7607 2789. www.unl.ac.uk/
Archives of the Roundhouse and Open Space Theatre. Books etc. to support university courses.

LONDON, Victoria & Albert Museum, Department of Prints etc., Cromwell Road, South Kensington, London, SW7 2RL. 020 7938 8617.
e-mail enquiries@nal.vam.ac.uk www.nal.vam.ac.uk
Material on the theatre in general, including posters and actors in character etc. Other parts of the Museum could be assistance to researchers.

LONDON, Waltham Forest Archives, Vestry House Museum, Vestry Road, Walthamstow, London, E17 9NH. 020 8509 1917.
e-mail vestry-house@al.lbwf.gov.uk www.lbwf.gov.uk
Material on Walthamstow Palace and other local theatres, amateur and professional, 19th century onwards.

LONDON, Wandsworth Museum, The Courthouse, 11 Garret Lane, London, SW18 4AQ. 020 8871 7074. www.wandsworth.museum@wandsworth.gov.uk
Limited amount of material on the Battersea Palace Theatre and the Balham Hippodrome.

LONDON, Westminster City Library, City of Westminster Archives Centre, 10 St Ann's Street, London, SW1P 2XR. 020 7641 5180. e-mail archives@westminster.gov.uk
Extensive collections of playbills, programmes etc. covering not only London, but also the rest of the UK, Dublin, Europe and the USA, mainly 19th century onwards.

LOWESTOFT RO, CL, Clapham Road, Lowestoft, Suffolk, NR32 1DR.
01502 405357. e-mail lowestoft.ro@libher.suffolk.cc.gov.uk
www.suffolkcc.gov.uk/libraries.
Collection of material relating to Lowestoft theatres, 18th century onwards.

LUTON Museum & Art Gallery, Wardown Park, Luton, Bedfordshire, LU2 7HA.
01582 546725. e-mail adeye@luton.gov.uk
Small collection of material relating to the Grand and Alma Theatres Luton.

MAIDSTONE Centre for Kentish Studies, Sessions House, County Hall, Maidstone, Kent ME4 1XQ. 01622 694363. e-mail archives@kent.gov.uk
Playbills, programmes etc. for Sandwich Theatre and other Kentish players and performances.

MANCHESTER John Rylands University Library of Manchester, 150 Deansgate, Manchester, M3 3EH. 0161 834 5343. www.rylib.man.ac.uk
Extensive collection of material on the theatre, both in Manchester area and nationally, 17th century onwards.

MANCHESTER CL Arts Library, Theatre Collection, St.Peter's Square, Manchester, M2 5PD. 0161 234 1900. e-mail dlt@libraries.manchester.gov.uk
Large collection of playbills, programmes etc. for Manchester theatres, including TR.

MARGATE LSD, Cecil Square, Margate, Kent, CT9 1RE. 01843 223626.
www.kent.gov.uk
Playbills, programmes etc. for TR, Winter Gardens and Grand/Hippodrome, 18th century onwards.

MATLOCK Derbyshire CRO, County Hall, New Street, Matlock, Derbyshire, DE4 3AG. 01629 580000. e-mail recordoffice@derbyshire.gov.uk
Playbills, programmes etc. for Derbyshire theatres, 19th century onwards.

MIDDLESBROUGH Cleveland Archives, Exchange House, 6 Marton Road, Middlesbrough, Cleveland, TS1 1DB. 01642 248321.
Collection of material on local theatres, including Stockton-on-Tees, 19th century onwards.

MIDDLESBROUGH CL, Victoria Square, Middlesbrough, Cleveland, TS1 2AY. 01642 729048. www.middlesbrough.gov.uk
Playbills, programmes etc., professional and amateur, for Middlesbrough, 19th century onwards.

MORDEN Merton LSD, Merton Civic Centre, London Road, Morden, Surrey, SM4 5DX. 0208545 3239. e-mail mertonlibs@compuserve.com
Material relating to the Wimbledon Theatres and amateur companies, 20th century.

NEWCASTLE-UPON-TYNE Newcastle City Libraries LSD, Princess Square, Newcastle, Tyne & Wear, NE99 1DX. 0191 261 4100/06.
e-mail heritage@newcastle.gov.uk
Extensive collection of playbills, programmes etc. for Newcastle theatres, including TR, 18th century onwards.

NEWCASTLE-UPON-TYNE Northumberland RO, Melton Park, North Gosforth, Newcastle, Tyne & Wear, NE3 5QX. 0191 236 2680.
www.swinhope.demon.co.uk/genuki/NBL
Material relating to various Northumberland theatres, 18th century onwards.

NEWCASTLE- UPON-TYNE Tyne and Wear Archives Service, Blandford House, Blandford Square, Newcastle, Tyne and Wear, NE1 4JA. 0191 230 2614.
e-mail twas@dial.pipex.com www.thenortheast.com/archives/
Extensive material on local theatres, music hall etc. in Newcastle and area, 18th century onwards.

NORTH SHIELDS LSD, Northumberland Square, North Shields, Tyne and Wear, NE30 1QU. 0191 200 5424. e-mail central@ntlib.demon.co.uk
Playbills, programmes etc. for North Shields and area theatres, 19th century onwards.

NORTHAMPTON CRO, Woottton Hall Park, Northampton, Northamptonshire, NN4 8BQ. 10604 762129. e-mail nro@northamptonshire.gov.uk
Collections of material relating to county theatres, including Northampton TR archives, 18th century onwards.

NORTHAMPTON Northamptonshire Studies Collection, CL, Abington Street, Northampton, NN1 2BA. 01604 462040. www.northamptonshire.gov.uk
Playbills, programmes etc. for county and TR Northampton theatres, 19th century onwards.

NORWICH Norfolk CRO, Gildengate Hose, Anglia Square, Upper Green Lane, Norwich, NR3 1AX. 01603 761349. email nro@norfolk.gov.uk www.archives.norfolk.gov.uk
Extensive collection of material on Norfolk theatres, including TR, 18th century onwards.

NORWICH LSD, CL, Gildengate House, Anglia Square, Upper Green Lane, Norwich, Norfolk NR3 1AX. 01603 215254. e-mail norfolk.studies@norfolk.gov.uk
Playbills, programmes etc. relating to Norfolk and Norwich theatres, mainly 19th century onwards.

NORWICH University of East Anglia Library, Archives Department, Norwich, Norfolk, NR4 7TJ. 01603 593491. www.lib.uea.ac.uk
Fisher Theatre Collection of material relating to the Fisher Theatre Circuit in Norfolk and Suffolk 1792-1844 and later, plus press cuttings for Norwich and Gt Yarmouth theatres.

NOTTINGHAM Nottinghamshire Archives, County House, Castle Meadow Row, Nottingham, NG2 1AG. 0115 958 1634. e-mail archives@nottscc.gov.uk www.nottscc.gov.uk/libraries/archives/index
Material relating to Playhouse and TR Nottingham.

NOTTINGHAM County Library LSD, Angel Row, Nottingham, NG1 6HP. 0115 915 2873. e-mail nottingham_local_studies@hotmail.com www.notlib.demon.co.uk
Playbills programmes etc. relating to Nottingham theatres, 18th century onwards.

NOTTINGHAM University Library, Department of Manuscripts, Univeresity Park, Nottingham, NG7 2RD. 0115 951 4565. www.mss.library.notttingham.ac.uk
Various manuscripts relating to theatre background. Books on history of the theatre.

OXFORD Bodleian Library, Broad Street, Oxford, OX1 3BG. 01865 277047. www.bodley.ox.ac.uk
Material relating mainly to the London theatre. A copyright deposit library.

OXFORD Oxfordshire Archives, County Hall, New Road, Oxford, OX1 1ND. 01865 815203. e-mail archives.occdla@dial.pipex.com www.oxfordshire.gov.uk
Oxford Playhouse records, 20th century.

OXFORD Oxfordshire CL, Centre for Oxfordshire Studies, Westgate, Oxford, OX1 1DJ. 01865 815749. e-mail cos@oxfordshire.gov.uk www.oxfordshire.gov.uk/culture Programmes, cuttings etc. for Oxford theatres, 19th century onwards and books on the theatre.

PLYMOUTH City of Plymouth Museum and Art Gallery, Drake Circus, Plymouth, Devon, PL4 8AJ. 01752 668000/304774. e-mail enquiry@plymouthmuseum.gov.uk www.plymouthmuseum.gov.uk Playbills, programmes etc. relating to Plymouth theatres, particularly TR, 19th century onwards.

PLYMOUTH CL Drake Circus, Plymouth Devon, PL4 8AL. 01752 305923. e-mail library@plymouth.gov.uk www.cyberlibrary.org.uk Programmes and related material for various Plymouth theatres 19th century onwards.

POOLE Poole Museum Service, Waterfront Museum, 4 High Street, Poole, Dorset, BH15 1BW. 01202 683138. e-mail museums@poole.gov.uk www.poole.gov.uk Material and ephemera for local theatres, 18th century onwards.

PORTSMOUTH Portsmouth CL LSD, Guildhall Square, Portsmouth, Hampshire, PO1 2DX. 01705 819311. e-mail reference.library@portsmouthcc.gov.uk Playbills, programmes etc. for Portsmouth and other theatres, 1800 onwards.

PRESTON Lancashire CRO, Bow Lane, Preston, Lancashire, PR1 2RE. 01772 263039. www. e-mail record.office@lancs.gov.uk www.lancashire.gov.uk/education/lifelong/ro Extensive material on Lancashire theatres, particularly Preston, Oldham, Blackpool and Barrow, 18th century onwards.

PRESTON Museum of Lancashire, Stanley Street, Preston, PR1 4YP. 01772 264075. e-mail museum@lancs.co.uk Programmes, posters etc. relating to Blackpool theatres, 20th century.

RAMSGATE Ramsgate Library LSD, Museum, Guildford Lawn, Ramsgate, Kent, CT11 9AY. 01843 593532. (these archives may have moved to Dover) www.kent.gov.uk/ramsgategallery Playbills, posters, ephemera for Ramsgate theatres, and TR Margate archives from 19th century.

READING Berkshire CRO, 9 Coley Avenue, Reading, RG1 6AF. 0118 901 5132.
email arch@reading.gov.uk
Archives of theatres and theatre companies in the county, 16th century onwards, some
relating to London.

READING British Broadcasting Corporation, Written Archives Centre, Caversham
Park, Reading, RG4 8TZ. 0118 9469281. e-mail WAC.enquiries@bbc.co.uk
The permanent written records of the BBC, possible correspondence with BBC actors

READING University, Centre for Ephemera Studies, 2 Earley Gate, Whiteknights,
PO Box 239, Reading, RG6 6AU. 0118 378 8770. e-mail library@reading.ac.uk.
www.library.rdg.ac.uk
A limited number of playbills and other ephemera, London and provinces.

REDRUTH Cornwall Cornish LSD, CL, 2-4 Clinton Road, Redruth, TR15 2QE.
01209 216760. e-mail cornishstudies@ library.cornwall.gov.uk
Cornish theatre material, 20th century.

RICHMOND The National Archives, Ruskin Avenue, Kew, Richmond, Surrey,
TW9 4DU. 020 8876 3444. www.nationalarchives.gov.uk
The papers of the Lord Chamberlain's Office, the licenser of theatres and plays and
theatre information in State Papers.

RICHMOND Richmond LSD, The Old Town Hall, Whittaker Avenue, Richmond,
Surrey, TW9 1PT. 020 8332 6820. e-mail localstudies@ richmond.gov.uk
www.richmond.gov.uk
Playbills, posters, programmes, cuttings etc. in local theatres including the TR Richmond.

ROCHDALE Arts and Heritage Centre LSD, Champness Hall, Drake Street Rochdale,
OL16 1PB. 01706 864915. www.gmcro.co.uk/reposit
Theatre material including posters etc. for local theatres, including TR Rochdale, 18th
century onwards.

ROYSTON Museum, 5 Lower King Street, Royston, Hertfordshire, SG8 5AL.
01763 242587, e-mail curator@roystonmuseum.org.uk
Programmes etc. for local amateur dramatic societies, from 1830s onwards.

RUTHIN Denbighshire CRO, 46 Clwyd Street, Ruthin, LL15 1HP. 01824 708250.
e-mail archives@denbighshire.gov.uk www.denbighshire.gov.uk
Playbills, programmes for theatres in the county including the TR Wrexham, 19th
century onwards.

SALFORD Local History Library, Peel Park, Salford, Greater Manchester, M5 4WU. 0161 736 2649. e-mailinfo@lifetimes.org.uk www.lifetimes.org.uk
Programmes, cuttings relating to Salford theatres.

SCARBOROUGH,North Yorkshire Library LSD, Vernon Road, Scarborough, YO11 2NN. 01723 364285. e-mail scarborough.library@northyorks.gov.uk
Programmes, handbills etc. for various Scarborough theatres, 19th century onwards.

SHEFFIELD National Fairground Archive, University of Sheffield, S10 2TN. 0114 222 7231. www.fairground@shef.ac.uk
Large amount of original material relating to fairs, circus and popular entertainments.

SHEFFIELD CL LSD, Surrey Street, Sheffield, S1 1XZ. 0114 273 4753. e-mail local studies@dial.pipex.com
Playbills, programmes, cuttings etc. for various Sheffield theatres, 19th century onwards.

SHEFFIELD City Museum, Weston Park, Sheffield, S10 2TP. 0114 278 2600. www.sheffieldgalleries.org.uk
Small number of posters etc. on Sheffield theatres and music halls.

SHREWSBURY Shropshire Records and Research Centre, Castle Gates, Shrewsbury, SY1 2AQ. 01743 255350. e-mail research@shropshire-cc.gov.uk
www.shopshire-cc.gov.uk/research.nsf
Playbills, posters etc. for theatres in Shrewsbury, Ludlow and Bridgnorth, 16th century onwards.

SOUTH SHIELDS South Tyneside CL, Prince George Square, South Shields, Tyne and Wear, NE33 2PE. 0191 427 1818. e-mail reference.library@tyneside mbc.gov.uk
www.s tynesidembc. gov.uk
Playbills, cuttings etc. on South Tyneside theatres, including TR South Shields, 19th century onwards.

SOUTHAMPTON Southampton Archives Service, Civic Centre, Southampton, SO14 7LY. 023 8083 2251. e-mail city.archives@southampton.gov.uk
Theatre programmes, mainly 20th century, for Southampton theatres.

SOUTHAMPTON University, Special Collections, Highfield, Southampton, SO17 1BJ. 01703 592721. e-mail archives@soton.ac.uk
Playbills etc. for theatres, mainly London, 19th century onwards.

SOUTHEND-ON-SEA. Essex RO, Southend Branch, CL, Victoria Avenue, Southend-on-Sea, Essex, SS2 6EX. 01702 612621. www.southend.gov.uk
Programmes etc. for Southend and area theatres, 19th century onwards.

STAFFORD Staffordshire RO and William Salt Library, 19 Eastgate Street, Stafford, ST16 2LZ. 01785 278379. e-mail staffordshire.record.office@staffordshire.gov.uk www.staffordshire.gov.uk/ archives/salt
Licenses and theatre records for Staffordshire theatres, 18th century onwards Playbills, programmes etc. for theatres in the Stoke area.

STOCKPORT CL LSD, Wellington Road South, Stockport, Greater Manchester, SK1 3RS. 0161 474 4530. e-mail central.library@stockport.gov.uk
Playbills, programmes, cuttings etc. for Stockport theatres.

STRATFORD-UPON-AVON Shakespeare Centre Library, Henley Street, Stratford-upon-Avon, Warwickshire, CV37 6QW. 01789 204016. www.shakespeare.org.uk
Very extensive collection on Shakespeare productions, players and locations, including archives of Shakespeare Memorial Theatre from 1879.

SUMMERBRIDGE Theatre Search Collection, The Lodge, Braisty Woods, Summerbridge, North Yorkshire, HG3 4DN. 01423 780497.
Stage machinery and technical theatre, architecture, patents, postcards and theatrical fires.

SUNDERLAND Museum and Art Gallery, Borough Road, Sunderland, Tyne and Wear, SR1 1RP. 0191 565 0723. e-mail info@twmuseums.org.uk www.twmuseums.org.uk
Playbills, posters etc. for Sunderland theatres, 18th century onwards.

SWANSEA South Wales Miners' Library, University of Wales Swansea, Hendrefoelon House, Gower Road, Swansea, West Glamorgan, SA2 7NB. 01792 518603. e-mail miners@swansea.ac.uk www.swan.ac.uk/lis/swml
Records relating to amateur productions by miners mainly at their institutes.

SWANSEA RL LSD, Alexandra Road, Swansea, West Glamorgan, SA1 5DX. 01792 516753. e mail swanlib@demon.co.uk
Playbills etc. relating to Swansea theatres, and index to *The Cambrian* newspaper from 1804.

SWANSEA West Glamorgan Archive Service, County Hall, Oystermouth Road, Swansea, West Glamorgan, SA1 3SN. 01792 636589. e-mail archives@swansea.gov.uk www.swansea.gov.uk /archives
Programmes, posters etc. for Swansea and area theatres, 20th century.

SWINDON CL LSD, Regent Circus, Swindon, Wiltshire, SN1 1QG. 01793 463240. e-mail swindonref@swindon.gov.uk www.swindon.gov.uk
Records relating to Swindon theatres.

TAUNTON Somerset RO, Obridge Road, Taunton, TA2 7PU. 01823 278805. e-mail somerset_archives@compuserve.com www.somerset.gov.uk
Playbills, posters etc. for Somerset theatres, 19th century onwards, also for some London theatres.

TORQUAY RL, Lymington Road, Torquay, Devon, TQ1 3DT. 01803 208305. e-mail reflib@torbay.gov.uk e-mail wsro@wiltshire.gov.uk www.wiltshire.gov.uk/heritage
Programmes etc. for Pavilion Theatre Torquay and professional and amateur productions in Torbay area, 20th century.

TROWBRIDGE Wiltshire and Swindon RO, Bythesea Road, Trowbridge, Wiltshire, BA14 8BS. 01225 713709/713732. e-mail trowref@compuserve.uk www.wiltshire.gov.uk
Playbills and theatre records for Wiltshire theatres, professional and amateur, 18th century onwards.

TRURO Cornwall CRO, County Hall, Truro, Cornwall, TR1 3AY. 01872 323127. e-mail cro@ceo.cornwall.gov.uk www.cornwall.gov.uk
Posters etc. for Cornish theatres, both professional and amateur, 19th century onwards.

TUNBRIDGE WELLS Museum and Art gallery, Civic Centre, Mount Pleasant, Tunbridge Wells, Kent, TN1 1JN. 01892 55471/526121. www.tunbridgewells.gov.uk
Playbills etc. the Tunbridge Wells Theatre, Opera House and Assembly Hall, 18th century onwards.

TWICKENHAM District Library, LSD, Garfield Road, Twickenham, Middlesex, TE1 3JS. 020 8891 7271 e-mail twicklib@richmond.gov.uk www.richmond.gov.uk (the collection may move to Richmond LSD)
Material relating to amateur theatre in the area.

UXBRIDGE Hillingdon PL Heritage Service, 14-16 High Street, Uxbridge, Middlesex, UB8 1HD. 01895 250702. e-mail clib@hillingdon.gov.uk www.hillingdon.gov.uk
Small collection of Uxbridge playbills and photographs, and scrapbook of 19th century reviews.

WAKEFIELD Museum, Wood Street, Wakefield, West Yorkshire, WF1 2EW. 01924 305351. www.wakefield.gov.uk/culture/museum
Playbills, programmes etc. for Wakefield theatres and Opera House, 18th century onwards.

WAKEFIELD West Yorkshire Archive Service, Newstead Road, Wakefield, WF1 2DE. 01924 305980. e-mail archives@wyashq.demon.co.uk www.archives.wyjs.org.uk
Records relating to county theatres, including TR Wakefield, 18th century onwards.

WALSALL Local History Centre, Essex Street, Walsall, West Midlands WS2 7AS. 01922 721305. e-mail localhistorycentre@walsall.gov.uk www.walsall.gov.uk/culturalservices/library
Playbills, posters programmes etc. for local theatres, professional and amateur, 19th century onwards.

WARRINGTON PL, Museum Street, Warrington, Cheshire, WA1 1JB. 01925 442892. e-mail library@warrington.gov.uk www.warrington.gov.uk
Playbills, programmes for Warrington theatres, including music hall, 18th century onwards.

WARWICK Warwickshire CRO, Priory Park, Cape Road, Warwick, CV34 4JS. 01926 412735. e-mail recordoffice@warwickshire.gov.uk www.warwickshire.gov.uk
Records relating to the theatre in Warwickshire and elsewhere, 17th century onwards.

WEYMOUTH RL, Great George Street, Weymouth, Dorset, DT4 8NN. 01305 762418. e-mail dorsetlibraries@dorsetcc.gov.uk
Playbills etc. for Weymouth, including TR, and Dorchester theatres, 18th century onwards.

WHITEHAVEN Cumbria CRO, Scotch Strret, Whitehaven, Cumbria, CA28 7BJ. 01946 852920. e-mail whitehaven.record.office@cumbriacc.gov.uk www.cumbria.gov.uk/archives
Records relating to TR and Empire Theatres Whitehaven.

WIGAN Wigan Heritage Service. The History Shop, Library Street, Wigan, Greater Manchester, WN1 1DQ. 01942 828020. e-mail heritage@wiganmbc.gov.uk
A few programmes, cuttings, etc. of theatres and music halls in the Wigan area.

WINCHESTER Hampshire CRO, Sussex Street, Winchester, Hampshire, SO23 8TH. 01962 846154. e-mail sadeax@hants.gov.uk ww.hants.gov.uk/record-office
Playbills, programmes for theatres in Hampshire and elsewhere, 18th century onwards.

WINCHESTER City Museum, Hyde Historic Resources Centre, 75 Hyde Street, Winchester, Hampshire SO23 7DW. 01962 848269.
e-mail museums@winchester.gov.uk. www.winchester.gov.uk/heritage/home
A limited number of posters relating to TR Winchester.

WINDSOR Eton College Library, Windsor, Berkshire, SL4 6DB.
01753 671221/269. e-mail archivist@etoncollege.org.uk
Small collection of material relating to leading theatre figures.

WOKING, Surrey History Centre, 130 Goldsworth Road, Woking, Surrey, GU21 1ND. 01483 594594. e-mail shs@surreycc.gov.uk www.she.surreycc.gov.uk
Playbills etc. relating to Surrey theatres and archive of Thorndyke Theatre Leatherhead.

WOLVERHAMPTON Archives and LSD, 42-50 Snow Hill, Wolverhampton, West Midlands, WV2 4AG. 01902 552480. www.wolverhampton.gov.uk/library/archives
Programmes etc. relating to Wolverhampton theatres, including TR, 19th century onwards.

WORCESTER Hereford and Worcester LSD, PL, Foregate Street, Worcester, WR1 1DT. 01905 765312. e-mail worcesterlib@worcestershire.gov.uk
www.worcestershire.gov.uk/libraries
Playbills, programmes etc. for the TR and Swan theatres, amateur productions, 19th century onwards.

WORTHING Museum and Art Gallery, Chapel Road, Worthing, West Sussex, BN11 1HD. 01903 39999. e-mail worthing_museum@breathemail.net
Programmes, posters, cuttings etc. relating to Worthing theatres, 19th century onwards.

YORK York PL, Museum Street, York, YO1 2DS. 01904 655631.
e-mail reference.library@york.gov.uk www.york.gov.uk
Playbills, programmes etc. for York theatres, 18th century onwards.

YORK York Minster Archives, Dean's Park, York, YO1 2JD.
01904 611118. www.york.ac.uk/services/library
Playbills, York and Yorkshire, 18th and 19th centuries.

LIBRARIES

Books on the theatre are an essential part of research, and libraries can be of assistance although holdings in a specific town may vary; some may contain little or nothing of value to family historians. However the libraries listed contain books on the theatre and related activity in various formats. Some are private organisations or specific to universities which may only be open to the public on certain conditions. Approaches to these libraries should be made prior to a projected visit and charges to use some of these libraries or their services may be made.

ABERDEEN Northern College of Education Library, Hilton Place Aberdeen,
AB24 4FA. 01224 283571. e-mail mail@abdn.ac.uk
Books to support university courses.

ABERYSTWYTH University of Wales, The Hugh Owen Library, Penglais. Dyfed,
SY23 3DZ. 01970 622396. e-mail info@abert.ac.uk www.inf.abert.ac.uk/locations/libraries
Books etc. on theatre.

BANGOR University College of North Wales Library, Bangor, LL57 2DG.
01248 382983. www.bangor.ac.uk
Books to support university courses.

BEDFORD De Montfort University, Lansdowne Campus Library, 37 Lansdowne
Road, Bedford, MK40 2BZ. 01234 793390. www.dmu.ac.uk

BIRMINGHAM Conservatoire Library, Paradise Place Birmingham, B3 3HG.
0121 3315915. e-mail mu.library@uce.ac.uk www.uce.ac.uk
Books on opera etc.

BRIGHTON University, St Peter's House Library, 16-18 Richmond Place, Brighton,
BN2 2NA. 01273 571820. www.silver.brighton.ac.uk
Books on theatre to support University courses.

CARDIFF Welsh College of Music & Drama Library, Castle Grounds, Cathays Park,
Cardiff, South Glamorgan, CF1 3ER. 029 2034 2854. e-mail agusjm@wcomd.ac.uk
www.library.wcomd.ac.uk
Books on drama and the theatre.

CHICHESTER Chichester Institute of Higher Education, Bishop Otter College, College Lane, Chichester, West Sussex, PO19 4PE. 01243 816089. www.chilhe.ac.uk Books to support courses on the theatre, ballet etc.

COLCHESTER University of Essex, Albert Sloman Library, Wivenhoe Park, Colchester, Essex, CO4 3SQ. 01206 873188. www.essex.ac.uk Collection of works to support the teaching of drama at the University.

COLERAINE University of Ulster Library, Comore Road, Coleraine, Northern Ireland, BT52 1SA. 01265 324546. www.ulster.ac.uk Books and periodicals relating to theatre and drama.

COVENTRY, University of Warwick CL, Gibbet Hill Road, Coventry, West Midlands, CV4 7AL. 024 7652 3033. e-mail library@warwick.ac.uk www.library.warwick.ac.uk Extensive collection of works on the theatre, British, European and North American.

DEVIZES, Wiltshire County Council, Music & Drama Library, Sheep Street, Devizes, Wilts, SN10 1DW. 01380 722633/726878. www.wiltshire.gov.uk/libraries Drama textbooks, playsets and pantomimes.

DORKING Surrey County Performing Arts Library, Vaughan Williams House, West Street, Dorking, Surrey, RH4 1BY. 013906 887509. www.surreycc.gov.uk/libraries Large collection of plays and books on drama and music.

EGHAM, Royal Holloway & Bedford New College Library, University of London, Egham Hill, Egham, Surrey, TW20 OEX. 01784 443123. www.lb.rhbnc.ac.uk Extensive library supporting one of the major drama departments in UK universities.

EXETER, University Library, Stocker Road, Exeter, Devon, EX4 4PT. 01392 263860. www.ex.ac.uk/library Drama book collection to support university courses.

GLASGOW University Library, Hillhead Street, Glasgow, Strathclyde, G12 8QE. 0141 3306797. www.gla.ac.uk/library/ Large collection of books on the performing arts to support university courses.

GLASGOW Royal Scottish Academy of Music & Drama Library, 100 Renfrew Street, Glasgow, Strathclyde, G2 3DB. 0141 332 4101. www. e-mail drlib@rsamd.ac.uk Extensive library of works on drama and performing arts.

GLOUCESTER Greyfriars Music & Drama Library, Greyfriars, Gloucestrer, Gloucestershire, GL1 1TS. 01452 426982. e-mail gfriars@gloscc.gov.uk
www.gloucestershire.gov.uk
Books on drama etc.

GUILDFORD School of Acting, 20 Buryfields, Guildford, Surrey, GU2 5DA. 01483 570593. e-mail enquiries@conservatoire.org.uk
Books on theatre and its history.

HATFIELD Hertfordshire Libraries, Performing Arts Library, New Barnfield, Travellers Lane, Hatfield, AL10 8XG. 01707 281533.
www.hertsdirect.org/infoasdvice/libraries
Books on theatre and performing arts.

LANCASTER University Library, Bailrigg, Lancaster, Lancashire, LA1 4YII. 01524 65201. www.lib.web.lancs.ac.uk.
Books etc. to support university teaching.

LEICESTER De Montfort University, Kimberlin Library, The Gateway, Leicester, Leicestershire, LE1 9BH. 0116 2577047. www.library.dmu.ac.uk
Books etc. to support university teaching.

LIVERPOOL John Moores University, Aldham Robarts Learning Resource Centre, Mount Pleasant, Liverpool, Merseyside, L3 5UZ. 0151 231 3104. www.livjm.ac.uk
Books etc. to support university teaching.

LONDON, Barbican Library, Barbican Centre, London, EC2Y 8DS. 020 7638 0569.
www.corpoflondon.gov.uk/barbican
A general public lending library with an extensive collection of books etc. on the performing arts.

LONDON, BBC Information Research Library, B256, Television Centre, London, W12 7RJ. 020 7765 3560. www.bbc.co.uk.
The Library offers a general reseach service on the performing arts, including the theatre.

LONDON, Central School of Speech and Drama Library, Embassy Theatre, Eton Avenue, London, NW3 3HY. 020 7559 3942. e-mail library@cssd.ac.uk
www.cssd.ac.uk
Printed material including biographies, periodicals and theatre postcards.

LONDON, Guildhall Library Printed Books Section, Aldermanbury, London, EC2 2EJ. 020 7332 1868. www.corpoflondon.gov.uk
Large specialist book collection on London theatres and actors.

LONDON, Garrick Club, Garrick Street, London, WC2E 9AY. 020 7836 1737.
A private club with a large collection of books on the theatre. Application in writing for specific areas of research.

LONDON, Guildhall School of Music & Drama Library, Barbican, London, EC2Y 8DT. 020 7382 7178. www.gsmd.ac.uk
Collection of books on the theatre including memoirs, in particular the circus. Not normally open to members of the public.

LONDON, Middlesex University Library, Trent Park, Bramley Road, Oakwood, Cockfosters, E14 4XS. 0181 362 6181. www.ilrs.mdx.ac.uk/lib
Drama and dance books for students studying performing arts.

LONDON, National Operatic & Dramatic Association Library, 1, Crestfield Street, London, WC1H 8AU. 020 7837 5655.
Books etc. related to the light musical theatre.

LONDON, Performing Arts Library, First Floor, Production House, 25 Hackney Road, London E2 7NX. 020 7749 4850.
Books and photos on general theatre subjects.

LONDON, Royal College of Music Archive, Prince Consort Road, London, SW7 2BS. 020 7589 3643. www.rcm.ac.uk.
Books etc. on the musical aspects of the theatre, opera, variety and the music hall.

LONDON, University of Surrey at Roehampton, Digby Stuart College, Roehampton Lane, London, SW15 5SZ. 020 8392 3765. e-mail edesk@roe.ac.uk
Books etc. on the theatre to support courses.

LONDON, Westminster RL, 35 St Martin's Street, London, WC2H 7HP.
020 7641 4636. www.westminster.gov.uk/libraries/gateway
Very extensive collection of books on the theatre in all its forms. Theatrical newspapers on microfilm.

MANCHESTER Royal Northern College of Music Library, 124 Oxford Road, Manchester, M13 9RD. 0161 907 5243. e-mail library@rncm.ac.uk www.library.rncm.ac.uk
General material on the performing arts, including music hall.

NORTHAMPTON Nene College Library, Boughton Green Road, Northampton, Northamptonshire, NN2 2AL. 01604 735500. www.nene.ac.uk
General collections of books on the theatre etc. to support teaching courses.

NOTTINGHAM Trent University Library, Dryden Street, Nottingham, Nottinghamshire, NG1 4FZ. 0115 941 8418. www.ntu.ac.uk
Academic library of books on performing arts.

PETERBOROUGH, Religious Drama Society of GB, 58-60, Lincoln Road, Peterborough, PE1 2RZ. 01733 565613. e-mail info@radius.org.uk. www.radius.org.uk
Books etc. on the religious theatre.

SIDCUP Rose Bruford College Library, Lamborbey Park, Burnt Oak Lane, Sidcup, Kent, DA15 9DF. 020 8308 2626. www.bruford.ac.uk/library
Books etc. on theatre and related arts.

STRATFORD-UPON-AVON Shakespeare Institute Library, University of Birmingham, Church Street, Stratford-upon-Avon, Warwickshire, CV37 6HP. 01789 293384.
Extensive book collection on the theatre, including New Shakespeare Company archive from 1962.

WAKEFIELD Library HQ, Music and Drama Collection, Balne Lane, Wakefield, West Yorkshire, WF2 ODQ. 01924 302229. e-mail libraries@wakefield.gov.uk www.wakefield.gov.uk/libraries
Books etc. on theatre and drama history.

WARRINGTON University College Library, Fearnhead, Warrington, Cheshire, WA2 0DB. 01925 494284. www.warr.ac.uk
Books etc. to meet needs of theatre and drama students.

WARWICKSHIRE County Library, Barrack Street, Warwick, CV34 4TH. 01926 412189/412194. e-mail warwicklibrary@warwickshire.gov.uk
Books etc. on the theatre.

TRACING THEATRICAL ANCESTORS - HOW IT CAN BE DONE

Richard Nelson Lee (1806-1872)

My family have lived in the East End of London for generations so I am pure bred 'cockney', a tradition which carries through to me for I was born in Hackney. My mother's name was Govey and tracing her father's side of the family back to the 18th century was not too difficult when I first set out on the task in the 1960s. Her mother's maiden name was Lee, a most common name and her birth certificate of the 1870s stated that her father had numerous first names - Victor Leopold Alexander Lee, a colourman of Bethnal Green. Her mother's maiden name was Mondrell, and there was only one Victor Lee (he died young in 1880 which accords with family knowledge) who married an Elizabeth Mondrell in the marriage indexes, in the right place, at the right time and which fitted with other verifiable facts.

Victor Lee's marriage certificate shows his father as Nelson Lee, whose occupation was "theatre manager". This came as a surprise when first discovered in 1967 as a theatre connection was not known in family folklore. How to find out more about him? I went to a reference library and on the off chance looked at a nineteenth century theatre dictionary and there he was, found at the first hurdle. Nelson Lee (1806-72), first name Richard, had been a harlequin, pantomime writer, and theatre manager. Not much more than this but on this basis he must have been well known, so I looked at the same time at the *Dictionary of National Biography* on the off chance that he was one of the great. Yet again to my surprise and that sudden joy experienced by most family historians, there he was again. From this and many other books, articles and original material, I found out that he was considered one of the leading three or four pantomime writers of its great hey day in the mid nineteenth century. As a young man he had been a harlequin and a fair ground showman and much else. Licensing records and documents at the Greater London Record Office show that he organised the great fair in London at the time of the coronation of Queen Victoria in 1837, where he made his first fortune. He lost it again at the fair he set up at the time of the Great Exhibition of 1851 which the wet weather made into a disaster.

Next I went to the Theatre Museum, now in Covent Garden but then located in the Victoria and Albert Museum. There I saw for the first time his handwriting made difficult to read no doubt by over use. It was a letter from Nelson (so named because it was claimed he was born on the day of Admiral Nelson's funeral though his birth has not been traced and he was without doubt illegitimate) advising another theatre manager about frauds at ticket offices, plus a photograph of the 1860s (called then a

Mr Nelson Lee, as Khuleborn the Water King.

carte de visite) showing him in a top hat and heavy overcoat. *The Era* for January 1872 was then consulted which gave a long obituary, plus other main theatrical newspapers of the time. The obituary was so detailed that it even mentioned the number of coffins in which he was buried at Abney Park Cemetery, Stoke Newington - light wood inner, then lead, then oak.

The next step was to look at the extensive collection of playbills held at the Guildhall Library, London, though there were other London collections; this was the most convenient. He was not difficult to locate him as he either appeared in, wrote or managed the pantomimes which traditionally opened at Christmas each year. His name regularly appeared in black lettering in the playbill advertisements, small at first in the 1830s, but by the 1860s they were very large as the inclusion of his name ensured a large audience. Reviews of pantomimes in newspapers, local and national (even in *The Times*) always appeared during late December so here was another source. The most prolific pantomime writer of his time, I was able to put together a list of his theatrical works, including melodramas, which came to nearly 250 in total. Allardyce Nicoll's monumental, *History of English Drama 1660-1900*, Cambridge University Press (several volumes, various dates) lists the plays, pantomimes etc. attributed to specific authors in each period; the volumes covering the first and second halves of the nineteenth century showed many under the name of Nelson Lee.

The text of most of his productions can be seen in the Lord Chamberlain's Collection Plays etc. at the British Library. The text of each theatre performance was submitted to the Lord Chamberlain who 'censored' them which covers the period 1843-1960 and there is a published index to the whole. Lee's writing was difficult to read so it was relief to find that many of his later offerings, which he both wrote and managed, were in the hand of his eldest son, Nelson James Lee. His will was also informative and showed that he owned numerous properties in Dalston, including the house he had built in 1850 in Shrubland Road Dalston and in which he died. Outside he erected a plaque stating 'Nelson's Cottage 1850'. Despite bomb damage and redevelopment the house and plaque remain to this day. It was even possible to get the London Borough of Hackney to erect a commemorative plaque to Lee in the 1990s on the outside of 67 Shrubland Road as one of the Borough's notable historic figures.

This research enabled me to write an article for a theatre journal published in the USA listing all his works, distinguishing them from those of his eldest son. I was able to obtain material from the Royal Archives at Windsor Castle for Lee had dedicated and published a small children's book in 1850 to a member of the Royal Family, by permission. In the 1990s the *Dictionary of National Biography*, where the account of Lee's life had been found, was being rewritten as part of the new *Oxford Dictionary of*

A DECLARATION.

I HEREBY PUBLICLY DECLARE, after Inventing and Writing Two Hundred and Eleven Comic Pantomimes, played in London and the principal Towns in England during a period of Thirty Years, that the one now performing with such astounding success at the City of London Theatre, entitled "ALONZO THE BRAVE, or HARLEQUIN and the FAIR IMOGINE," is not only the Best I have Written, but the most complete in construction.

FURTHER MORE I DECLARE, the TRANSFORMATION SCENE, announced as the "Valley of Ferns and Fairy Foxgloves," Designed and Painted by Mr. W. BEAUMONT, the Mechanism by Mr. JOHN BURKETT, is the Best I have ever witnessed during my lengthened career, far surpassing even the palmy days of Madme. VESTRIS, so famous for Scenic Representations.

The Public's Obedient Servant,

4, NELSON'S COTTAGES,
SHRUBLAND ROAD,
DALSTON.

NELSON LEE.

OFFICIAL INFORMATION.—The Box Office is open from Eleven till Four, and the Stage Door Entrance at Half-past Five o'Clock, by which the Crowd can be avoided. The Pantomime concludes a little after Nine, in time for Trains.

Printed by W.'NOWELL's (late Peel's) Steam Machine, 74, New Cut Lambeth, and at Brixton.

National Biography. I was asked to rewrite the entry for my great great grandfather, a rare family history pleasure.

Most of the sources covering the nineteenth century cited in this book were used, in particular A.E. Wilson, *East End Entertainment*, 1954, T. Frost, *The Old Showman and the Old London Fairs*, 1874, M. Williams, *Some London Theatres Past and Present*, 1883; and the *Era Almanac* 1868. Even the University of Texas at Austin was able to supply a photocopy of a letter written to Lee by Charles Dickens. The plans for the fairs he set up in 1837 and 1851 in central London were examined at the Greater London Record Office (now the LMA). But perhaps my best find was a published description of Nelson Lee, by a commentator of the 1850s:

'I often think with gratitude of the famous Mr. Nelson Lee - the author of I don't know how many hundreds of glorious pantos - walking by the summer wave perhaps, revolving in his mind the idea of some new gorgeous spectacle of faery, which the winter shall see complete and be a serving of New Panto.'

Who wrote this? - none other than William Makepeace Thackeray! Not all family historians who find the title 'actor' in the occupation box on an ancestor's certificate will be able to be as successful in locating detail as I have been. My quest has been exciting and is a continuing one, and already it has stretched over thirty years. If time permits I am considering preparing a biography of Nelson Lee, an indomitable nineteenth century showman.

Harry Champion (1865-1942)

Harry Champion was one of the most famous music hall performers of his time, singing songs associated with his name like 'Any Old Iron' and 'Boiled Beef and Carrots' one after the other at a ferocious speed. Accounts of his life and times appear in several theatrical books, though not in the *Dictionary of National Biography*. However this has now been rectified as it now appears in the *Oxford Dictionary of National Biography*, an entry which I prepared in 1996.

In my researches, first I went to the national newspapers for January 1942 and found that Harry Champion had an obituary in most of them. He had lived in Tottenham for decades so the local newspapers in that area added a few more. The British Library Newspaper Collection enabled me to follow up reference to him, as well as obituaries, in theatrical journals. The Theatre Museum could not help at all, as the only item they had about him was a Christmas card he had sent (this was rectified at a later date). The British Music Hall Society was very helpful as I was sent, among other things, No. 26 of the series *Music Hall*, published by Tony Barker in 1982. This is a detailed account of his life in over fifty pages, which stated that his real name was William Henry Crump.

This was followed by looking through the accounts of the history of the music hall in Westminster Reference Library which included R. Busby, *British Music Hall, an illustrated who's who*; S.T. Felstead, *Stars who made the halls*; W.M. Pope, *The Melody Lingers On*; P. Davison, *Songs of the British Music Hall*; M.W. Disher, *Winkles and Champagne*; R. Hudd, *Music Hall Personalties*. I also found that the BBC Sound Archives and the National Sound Archive have about 80 recordings of his performances some dating from 1911, which can now be listened to through the world wide web, and Harvard College Theater Library in the USA had prints of him in his distinctive stage dress.

However it was clear from the start that basic genealogical information was lacking. His marriage and the birth of his children were easily located from the biographical works, but his date of birth could not be found. William Crump, alias Harry Champion was a private man and revealed to nobody his exact origins. After extensive research, even following contact with his family, the results were inconclusive. The date of birth amongst the various certificates could only be given as 'probably' 8 April 1865 at 30 Grafton Street, Mile End, London. Family historians may find their entertainer ancestors surround their early life in mystery for a variety of reasons.

Harry Champion's date of death, 14 January 1942, was shown everywhere and although it was claimed his real name was William Henry Crump, the connection between the two was not proved from a contemporary source, which was needed to meet the exacting standards of the *Oxford Dictionary of National Biography*. The strategy I adopted to find this connection was to carry out a blanket search of all the local newspapers for the Tottenham area at the Newspaper Library. This was done in conjunction with my wife and nothing was found but references to Harry Champion alone. About to give up, my wife started to browse in the *Tottenham and Weekly Herald*, a weekly newspaper which has long ceased its separate existence. Limited in size due to wartime restrictions in newspaper supply, my wife was browsing and had reached the issue of 30 January 1942. Her eye was scanning the condolences column, and there it was! 'The family of William Henry Crump, otherwise known as Harry Champion, gives thanks for all the expressions of regret...' The connection was found which shows that straying off the main research and looking generally, not a recommended course of action, can sometimes pay dividends.

The entry was brought up-to-date by including the reference taken from a modern popular song book that Peter Sellers sang one or more of the songs that W.H. Crump, alias Harry Champion, made so popular before and during the First World War.

INDEX

Applause database 37

Backstage 32, 37
Bibliographies 17
Biographies 15-17
Books on the theatre 3, 8, 12, 14, 16, 17, 18, 19, 20, 23, 24, 27, 28, 29, 37
British Music Hall Society 27, 33-34
British Newspaper Library 8, 13, 23
British Theatre Museum 31

Champion Harry 6, 24, 76-77
Circuits 16
Circuses 21-23

Directory of Performing Arts Resources 37

ENSA and CEMA 35-36
Era, The 13-14, 16, 23, 32

Fairs 21-23

Histories 15-17

Irish theatre 6, 28-29

Lee Richard Nelson 22, 72-75
Licensing records 2
Lord Chamberlain 4, 5, 7, 74

Mander and Mitchenson collection 32-33
Music Hall 6, 18, 24-27, 29, 34
Musicals 7
National Theatre 7

Obituaries 14

Pantomime 5, 27-28
Picture libraries 34-35
Playbills 10-12
Play titles 16-17

Scottish theatre and music hall 27, 29-30
SIBMAS 37
Society for Theatre Research 31
Sound Archive 34

Theatre Notebook 31
Theatre Royal system 5
Theatres, minor 5
Theatres, London and regional 18-20
Theatrical benevolent funds 33
Theatrical newspapers 13-15
Theatrical programmes 10
Trade Unions 34

USA collections 32

Variety and vaudeville 6

Who's Who in the Theatre 15-16